# PROSPERITY'S
# 7 LINK CHAIN

# PROSPERITY'S

# 7 LINK CHAIN

## Chas Stevenson

Stevenson
ministries

Published by:
STEVENSON MINISTRIES
PO Box 421236, Houston, TX 77242
www.stevensonministries.org

Book design, cover design, interior design by Stevenson Ministries
Editors: Joni Stevenson, Dawn Kopa, Delia Prince
Cover: Patrick McGraw

Published in the United States of America

ISBN: 978-1506153322

# CONTENTS

# INTRODUCTION
# DOING MONEY RIGHT

Miracles don't cause prosperity. Principles do.

When I was a teenager, several of us had four wheel drive trucks so we could get in and out of the obscure hunting and fishing spots. Oh, and also so we could go fling mud all over everything after a good rain and then drive to school with our proof of "manhood". But inevitably, at some point about every year, one of the trucks would get stuck and another truck would have to pull it out. And no matter how strong the saving truck was, it always boiled down to the anticipation of, *is the chain going to hold*? No matter its length, and no matter how solid the frames on each end were, if just one link of the chain was weak or broken, our fun was over.

I've found that connecting to God is the same way. God wants to pull us up out of financial lack and into His covenant of prosperity and success. But between us is the all-important "chain". True Bible prosperity requires that several essential money principles must be known, believed, and done right. Think of it like a chain of seven connected Biblical truths that assure our strength from above. And just like with any chain, if only one link of the chain is missing or broken—if we're neglecting a principle—we find ourselves groping around for God, disconnected from His financial help, and usually infected with subtle, perpetual uncertainty

1

about our financial future. I want to help you end that. Though a miracle can give us a shove in the right direction, real wealth requires that every link is secure.

So, this book is about the Christian and his money. But rather than some get-rich-quick nonsense, it's about attitude, perception, belief, and lifestyle. For most of us, our attitudes on money and wealth were shaped by the world. They were shaped by our upbringing. They were shaped by how our parents and family thought about, talked about, and handled money. So we likely weren't brought up thinking about money *God's way*. Either our mentality was formed in the rut of poverty—poverty thinking, poverty planning, poverty worrying, poverty hoarding, poverty purchasing, or just plain ole broke. Or, we were brought up in a wealthy family that trusted money, loved money, and feared losing money so much that it unknowingly became lord to them. Both of those make people slaves to money. So for born again people who are now learning to live in the Kingdom of God, we need an attitude adjustment. If we don't get our attitude straightened out—if we don't get Kingdom-trained about money—if we don't fix the inside of us, we'll never experience true prosperity. Because prosperity begins on the inside.

The Church has come quite a long way. Whereas once Christians were wrongly taught that being poor and broke was "of God" and meant we were humble and content, now we honestly admit that poor people can have great pride, and broke people are usually very discontent. Whereas once the scripture was commonly misquoted as being "money is the root of all evil", now we know that it's actually written "the *love* of money is the root of all evil" (1 Timothy 6:10). Many of us have learned the Kingdom principle of sowing, reaping, giving, and "tithing".    And we've made the Scriptural discovery that there is a prosperity facet in our covenant with God. That means that it's actually *of God* to be prosperous rather than poor.

But somehow, so many believers are still finding divine prosperity very elusive. Even after years of faithful tithing and giving, some keep finding "holes in their buckets". And that's the reason for this book—we're going to plug the holes. Certainly, sowing finances into the Kingdom of God is part of receiving a harvest, but there is more to it—seven distinct links in the chain.

This real prosperity does not begin with a certain amount in mind, or end goal, of riches. It has nothing to do with the bottom line. It has everything to do with principle. The Bible says several times that "...the righteous shall live by faith" (Romans 1:17). Living by faith means that we live by our belief system. It means we learn right things about God. We believe those things. Then we act on those things. It means our lifestyle is shaped by the knowledge we affirm is from God. It means our thinking is shaped by God's Word. It means our attitude about life, about God, about everything, is to be persuaded to match the attitude of heaven. If we live a principled life based on God's Word, we are secure. If we can faithfully implement these seven money principles into our heart and lives, there is no possibility of financial lack or failure.

Are we faithful with money—how we think of it, how we earn it, how we spend it, and how we save it? If we can get reliable with it, God will get involved in it. God would love to be involved in our finances, as He desires to provide for us abundantly. But to do that, He needs to be able to touch our money. And to do *that*, He needs to touch how we *perceive* money. Most people think that the solution to their money problems is just to get more income, so they hope and pray for it. But it's bigger than that. And until we get some things straight, God just doesn't seem to sign off on our wage increase.

You see, spiritual things may be a higher priority to God, but to grow us spiritually, God requires faithfulness with natural things. Material things are our proving ground for spiritual things. If God can get hold of our attitude and lifestyle of this most essential part of our natural life, He can get hold of our spiritual life. If He can trust us with money, He can trust us with His Kingdom. "Therefore if you have not been faithful in the unrighteous mammon (material wealth), who will commit to your trust the true riches?" (Luke 16:11). Our spiritual lives suffer when our *material* life isn't ordered by principle. On the other hand, a secure foundation of *doing money right* will, in turn, launch us into true riches.

But please keep this in mind as you read: we must understand, believe, and expect the right things to come to pass in our life, *without really desiring wealth*. I know it sounds a bit tricky, but I believe many Christians have messed themselves up by hearing the prosperity message and running off to get rich. The Bible warns us against that. "Those who *desire to be rich* fall into temptation and a snare, and into many foolish and harmful lusts which drown men in destruction and perdition" (1 Timothy 6:9). Though we can prove Biblically that wealth is supposed to be part of a righteous man's life, we've got to disconnect from a *pursuit* of it. Though we know that riches are the result, we can't get caught desiring them or we'll get messed up. And realize that "rich" is a relative term, so rather than compare our level of wealth to someone else's, let's think of "rich" as *having a full supply.*

It's time to do money *right.*

# PROSPERITY LINK #1
# ELIMINATE THE POVERTY MENTALITY

I always have plenty. Always. No matter the need, whether big or small, I can say with certainty that the supply always comes. If I want to buy it, I can. If I want to give it, I've got it to give. If I need to do something, I do it. And I've got no anxiety about anything. I never worry, because I know God. He is my source. I think that way. I act that way. I have my "wants" in check. I go about life without a financial care in the world. And it has nothing to do with the bank account amount, but everything to do with a certain spiritual, supernatural consciousness of God's Word in my life. This is my mentality in Christ. And it's what God has envisioned for everyone.

*What's going on inside me?* That's what we have to ask first, for whatever is on the inside of us is what our life turns out to be. "Out of the heart proceed the issues of life" (Proverbs 4:23). Out of the heart comes our future. God has designed this life of faith to require our spirit man to possess things before our natural man is allowed to. The soul is a complex storehouse of our past, present, and future existence. And it determines everything. Jesus said not to go chasing things around, "See here! or See there! For indeed, the Kingdom of God is *within you*" (Luke 17:21). God's Kingdom is inside us. It is the same with our power for life and circumstance. Don't look on the outside for signs of possibility. Look on the inside. Prosperity begins on the inside of us. Our soul must begin see things clearly. Our soul must spend time seeking the Kingdom of God and His righteousness, so that the most prominent image in our mind concerning finances is God's great covenant of provision. If we catch our souls tumbling round and round with quiet desperation about our financial situation, we must realize that we're hindering God and delaying our victory.

Jesus said that out of the heart can proceed either evil things and evil thoughts or good things and good thoughts. Poverty is evil. Poverty kills. Poverty steals. Poverty ruins dreams, stifles hopes, and disrupts families. So troublesome thoughts of lack can't be allowed to exist inside us. Rather than quiet desperation and deferred hopes about money, we've got to pack our heart and soul with right things (from God's Word).

My mom tells me that when I was a child, we were at a retail store and I was pleading for her to buy me some toy. Her response was, "We don't have the money for that." And my response was, "Well, then write a check." To me, a checkbook meant all things were always possible and we had no lack. On some level, you could say I had a *prosperous* mentality. That is, until I began to understand "the system". And though my parents did a pretty good job of protecting me from it, a feeling of lack crept in here and there. And I would say that's what happened to many of us. We grew up with a life attitude and viewpoint of "not having enough"—a poverty mentality. Most of us grew up without great riches. We have, more or less, a history of poverty in our minds, and therefore we have money habits and money thoughts that don't line up with God's Word. And it takes concerted effort to change that. It takes diligent Bible time, prayer time, and meditation time to change our outlook from empty to full— from not enough to *I'm certain I'll always have more than enough since God cares for me.* It's not a checkbook that makes all things possible. It's God's Book.

Our self-perception (how we view ourselves) has a big part to play in the level of life we experience, "As a man thinks in his heart, so is he" (Proverbs 23:7). The startling fact is that 90 percent of our self-concept is formed by age twelve. Now think back to the mood and the subtle undercurrents of your first twelve years of life. It might explain a lot. My wife's nephew is a good, simple example. Up until he was a teenager, he had this testimony, "I hate pecans." But one day, my wife ordered him a pecan-filled dessert at a restaurant. He gobbled it up, ranting how good it was the whole time. In the car, my wife verified how much he really liked it, and then informed him that it had pecans in it. His response was, "But I hate pecans." And then it all came clear. His "I hate pecans" identity was not even real. It was only a self-concept he had formed because his mother hated pecans and said it out loud all the time. He had never really even formed his own opinion of pecans, but was only "parroting" what his mother said. We do the same with how we handle life and money—we just "parrot" what we've seen and heard.

People tend to look at *who deserves what* based on outward circumstance and need, but God is more moved by what's on the inside of us, "Man looks at the outward appearance, but the LORD looks at the heart" (1 Samuel 16:7). God answers the largeness (or smallness) of our heart.

What we need to do is get an internal image of "cup runneth over" (Psalm 23:5). Think "good measure, pressed down, shaken together, and running over" (Luke 6:38). And think "twelve baskets left over" after starting with one basket and feeding 5,000 men and their families (Matthew 14:20). How big does our heart trust Him? How much can we handle? If we have a thimble sized capacity to trust Him for finances, He can overflow our thimble. But if we can enlarge our heart's hopefulness, expectancy, and confidence toward God about money, we can turn our thimble into a bucket or a truck. And God can overflow that.

# IS IT GOD'S WILL THAT WE PROSPER?

The first question to answer is, *Is prosperity God's will?* As we look to the scriptures for the answer, keep in mind that our definition of 'prosperity' is important. Prosperity does not directly refer to an *amount* of money. Prosperity is not about the bottom line, nor some arbitrary goal of one million or something. Again, we can't look at a bank account to determine if we're prosperous. We must look to God's Word, and then be sure that His Word translates to a certain demeanor on the inside of us. Prosperity carries with it an attitude of triumph and confidence, regardless of the situation. It is said that in order for a football team to win a championship, they have to feel worthy in their own minds to do so. It's similar with prosperity—we need a sense of worth and favor from our Heavenly Father.

Once prosperity takes shape on the inside of us, on the outside it translates to having enough and then some. It's about God caring for us, but with extra so we can care for others. It's about abundance. It's about overflow. It's about God providing in every way, all the time, absolutely, without a doubt, for each of His people. Prosperity means that whatever level of financial life and responsibility you are in right now, you have more than enough—enough for the Kingdom, enough for yourself, enough for the poor, and enough to put in store. It doesn't mean we're sitting on loads of cash all the time, but rather that if we need the cash, God sees to it.

It is the will of God that we all prosper in all things. The apostle John gave us the express will of God by the Spirit, "Beloved, I pray that you may prosper in all things and be in health, just as your soul prospers" (3 John 2). John didn't pray for people to be poor and sick, but prosperous and well. But again, that happening is dependent on whether or not our *soul* is prospering—the mind and consciousness part. Are we wealthy on the inside? Are we happy on the inside? Are we hopeful and confident on the inside? Are we pure and content on the inside? Are we certain of God's good will and promise to provide abundantly for us? Is our soul healthy and renewed by God's Word? In order to prosper, it has to be.

God is our profit instructor. Not only does He *not mind* us succeeding and having plenty, He wants to help us do it. "I am the Lord your God who teaches you to profit, Who leads you by the way you should go" (Isaiah 48:17).

Throughout the Bible, when men and women walked with God and sought Him with their whole heart, God caused them to prosper. "And the Lord was with Joseph, and he was a prosperous man. And his master saw that the Lord was with him, and that the Lord made all that he did to prosper" (Genesis 39:2-3). Concerning King Uzziah, "as long as he sought the Lord, God made him to prosper" (2 Chronicles 26:5).

> "Blessed is the man who fears the Lord, who delights greatly in His commandments. His descendants will be mighty on earth; The generation of the upright will be blessed. Wealth and riches will be in his house, And his righteousness endures forever" (Psalm 112:1-3).

In the New Testament, we are commanded to do the same thing and get the same results, "Seek first the Kingdom of God and His righteousness, and all these things shall be added unto you" (Matthew 6:33). Rather than seek the things and have neither the things nor the Kingdom, seek God and have both. Seeking God's Kingdom means to learn His Word and His way of being and doing.

Wealth and riches are promised to be in the righteous man's house. It's supposed to be true for every one of us who walk with God. If we seek His will, His Word, and His person, we will succeed.

> "This Book of the Law shall not depart from your mouth, but you shall meditate in it day and night, that you may observe to do according to all that is written in it. For then *you will make your way prosperous, and then you will have good success*" (Joshua 1:8).

Notice the emphasis, that *you* will make your way prosperous. And notice how success and prosperity are tied to our keeping the Word in our heart and in our mouth. It matters what we believe. It matters what we meditate on. It matters what internal conversation is going on inside us. And it matters what we say out of our mouth. If we allow thoughts of, *If I only had a bit more* to linger in us, we won't succeed. We've got to catch the deceptions of the enemy and cast them out.

Someone once asked a wealthy person if he felt like he was rich. He replied, 'No.' The person asked, "Well, how much would you need to feel rich?" The wealthy person replied, "Just a little bit more." Poverty thoughts can make even a wealthy person discontent. And poverty words spoken are contrary to the blessing and Word of God and can stop a whole family in their financial tracks.

## You Might Have A Poverty Mentality If

The word 'prosperity' is from a combination of two Greek words, 'pro' (being positive and for something) and 'spes' (hope). Prosperity means having a hopeful attitude and outlook in all things. And it leaves no room for pessimistic discouragement that is blind to the blessing, empty in its eye sight of God our Provider, and perpetually focused on what it *doesn't* have. Did you catch that? A lean toward pessimism is a clear sign of the poverty mentality.

Sometimes we're not even aware of how deep this poverty temptation is ingrained in us. It can be very subtle, so here is a self check-up on some things to look for and some solutions to practice breaking the poverty mentality.

1. If you're known as a "cheapskate" or a "penny-pincher", you might have a poverty mentality.

2. If you "strain at a gnat and swallow a camel" (Matthew 23:24), you might have a poverty mentality. That means you nit-pick the small things while over-indulge on the big things. For example, if you drive around fifteen minutes looking for the cheapest gas price in the city, finally find a place that saves you $.03 per gallon, and feel satisfied even though you used more gas money than you saved (not to mention your valuable time). Or for example, you put the milk back on the shelf at the grocery store because you forgot your $0.10 coupon, but yet you always own the latest model cell phone.

3. If you notice the tires on your car have just a couple of pieces of steel exposed, and your thought is "I can go a little bit longer on these", you might have a poverty mentality. Please, get some new tires.

4. If you can't bear to waste even the tiniest drop of shampoo, and spend ninety seconds shaking and pumping and then diluting with water your $.02 worth of product, you might have a poverty mentality. Now, if there is no more shampoo in the house, then do what you've got to do. But don't let it be because you can't bear to waste a drop of product. God is not afraid of spilling a little, of letting some crumbs fall to the ground, or of leaving some "corners in the field" for the poor.

(At this point, let me address the argument of "Well, we're supposed to be good stewards, right?" Yes, but not motivated from a position of lack. And what about being a good steward of our time? There was a time when I refused to pay someone to cut my grass. My rationale was that I had plenty of spare time, so I would do it myself. But the time came when I realized that my schedule was full and the value of my time in the ministry was worth more than the $30 it cost to hire someone.)

5. It's the same with your toothpaste: if you injure your fingers trying to squeeze that last bit of paste onto your brush, you might have a poverty mentality. Here's some good practice for you: while there is ample toothpaste still in the tube, throw it away, open a new one, and break off that poverty spirit!

6. If you save leftover food in the name of starving kids around world, you might have a poverty mentality. A poverty mentality causes people to feel guilty for having something that another person doesn't. But they're forgetting God. It is God's pleasure to bless people, and the only response necessary is praise and thanks for it. The guilt factor comes when people don't acknowledge God for their blessing and don't understand the prosperity covenant, which is exclusive for those in Christ who learn of it and have faith in Him for it.

7. If you find yourself saying, "Well, it'd sure be nice if our harvest would come in", you might have a poverty mentality. That could be evidence that you are speaking from a lack-filled heart,

with possibly a bit of a little grievance toward the Lord, who is waiting for you to get your heart and soul right about it.

8. If you are a socialist, or have socialist tendencies of wanting everyone to have equal wealth for *unequal* knowledge, ability, and effort, you might have a poverty mentality. Socialism is birthed out of covetousness, eyeballing someone else's stuff and thinking they owe it to you or someone else, ignoring God's system of value for work and services rendered. People can certainly willingly *give* their stuff if they wish. But it's absolutely wrong to "Robin Hood" it away from them and give to another.

9. If you consider a wealthy person and think, *They don't need all that*, or *They should give some away*, or *They shouldn't have spent so much on that thing*, you might have a poverty mentality. That is called "managing other people's money." And it is not of God.

10. If you have a strong dislike of or grudge against rich people, you might have a poverty mentality.

11. If you find yourself saving all your best things instead of using and enjoying them, you might have a poverty mentality. I once had a poverty mentality that showed up in my closet. I had this habit of being very selective when and how much I wore my nicest and favorite shirts. I tried to save them for special occasions, and in doing so, all it meant was that I didn't wear them very often. How ridiculous. Wear your favorites. Use your favorite stuff. Prosperity knows there's

always more where that came from. Poverty mentality, on the other hand, is scared to lose the thing it has.

12. If you have a hard time parting with your money for good and necessary things, you might have a poverty mentality. Early in my traveling ministry, I was pumping gas into my truck, and I caught myself calculating exactly how much I could afford to put in at the moment to get me to my next preaching meeting. My funds operated close to the zero level at the time, and gas prices had gone up dramatically. And I caught myself feeling anxious about it. But then I remembered that God is my source and that I'm better than a flower and better than a bird, and if He provides for them, He'll provide for me. So once and for all, I made a faith decision to settle the fact that gas is a necessity to complete my assignment in life and that from that day forward, I would always pump a full tank of gas and never think a second thought about it. I did it, and God has supplied. The poverty spirit was broken.

13. If you find yourself daydreaming about winning the lottery, you might have a poverty mentality. The lottery is not God's plan to prosper us, so quit playing it. I was standing in line at a store one day with the guy in front of me buying lottery tickets. I leaned over and said to him, "You're just wasting your money. You're not going to win anyway, so you might as well give that money to God." He looked at me and said, "You know, you're right."

14. If you rallied with the "99%" protesters against Wall Street, you might have a poverty mentality.

There will always be rich people. We'll always have the poor with us (Mark 14:7). And there will always be God's business system, which means there will *never* be equality of substance. It's God who gives power to get wealth, so stop blaming it all on some conspiracy. And we have to be logical about it. Most poor people are in no place to handle millions of dollars nor major corporations, nor provide thousands of jobs for people around the world. Many poor people aren't wise in their money management, nor are they educated in large capital economics, so it would be absurd to give them responsibility for money that they can't handle. But somebody needs to handle it. Therefore, it stays with the wealthy educated people. Why is that so hard to accept? And why is that such a big deal? It shouldn't be.

15. If most of your money decisions are fear based, you might have a poverty mentality. Realize that God doesn't partner with us in our fears, but rather in our faith.

16. If you won't set up "auto-pay" for standard monthly bills because you're scared there won't be enough in your account, you might have a poverty mentality. By setting things up for automatic draft, you can avoid the occasional late penalty when you misplace the bill or forget to write the check, plus save yourself some valuable time, plus save money on a stamp. And if you're still driving around town to the water company, cell phone company, and electric company to pay your bills in person, you are certainly not prepared to break the poverty cycle. All you're doing is wasting time

and gas because you haven't taken the time and effort to become efficient with your finances.

17. If you are paying for something in a store, and a few nickels and quarters spill out of your pocket or purse and start bouncing away, and you go after them like a dog after a bone, you might have a poverty mentality. Relax. Look at it as blessing someone else who needs to *find* some money. In the Old Testament, Israel was commanded to not go back into the harvest field to pick up a forgotten sheave, but to leave it for the poor. Applying that same principle at the grocery store may help you break poverty in your life.

18. If you have a lot of villains in your life—if criticizing and blaming others for everything that went wrong is your mode of operation, then you are victimizing yourself and might just have a poverty mentality. Take charge of your life. Take responsibility for your life. You cannot change what you are not responsible for. It's not your DNA, nor your generational history, nor even the economy's fault that you have missing links in the chain. For example, we golfers find ourselves looking for the villain in our golf game. But after a while, we all must acknowledge the big news flash. It's not the golf club's fault, nor the golf shoes' fault, nor the golf ball's fault. It's the golf *person's* fault. Buying better gear doesn't fix our crooked swing.

19. If you are on government subsidy of some sort and have no plans to get off of it, you might have a poverty mentality. I realize people go through tough seasons and need help, and it's true that some grow up in "the system" and have a hard

time getting out. But getting through the tough times and getting out of the system is a must. Learn to trust God. Use your faith, get on your feet, get a job, and break the cycle.

20. If every new business idea or work endeavor or brainstorm begins with "but we don't have the money for that", you might have a poverty mentality. Budgeting is good and necessary for the most part, but don't let the budget get the final word in. New endeavors must sometimes begin with a step outside our comfort zone. When God gets involved, things may not first appear to add up on paper, but we've got to leave some room for His supernatural work to do what it does. This does not mean to go on a presumptuous spending frenzy and take on unsubstantiated debt. But as we'll discuss in a later chapter, it refers to a faith life of letting the vision and the goal drive the finances rather than the other way around.

21. If you don't have a checking account, you might have a poverty mentality. It's impossible to do efficient business these days without one. Also, if you don't have a savings account, you might still have a poverty mentality. It means you aren't planning on ever having extra.

22. If, when you finally get some extra money, or when payday comes, you instantly gobble it all up, you might have a poverty mentality. Also the opposite—if you hoard it all up out of fear, you might still have a poverty mentality.

23. If you've stopped learning, if you rarely invest in books or online training courses for personal or spiritual growth, yet you're always eating out at

restaurants, you might have a poverty mentality. A prosperous person realizes the value of growing and learning and is not afraid to invest in themselves.

Complainers, pessimists, contrarians, and "Negative Nancies" almost always find themselves with this broken link. This poverty mentality is the spin of the unsaved world around us. It is a depressing, stressful attitude of striving all their lives to retire with just enough social security to get by in the end. We are to be different. And it starts on the inside with our thinking. "Do not be conformed to this world, but be transformed by the renewing of your mind" (Romans 12:2).

## BREAKING THE POVERTY MENTALITY

Early in our marriage and ministry, Joni and I would sometimes find ourselves on Friday night with hardly any extra money for anything. It would almost feel a bit threatening, but then we'd laugh it off and start heading out to a restaurant for date night. We just went and ate a fun meal to *spite the lack* right in its face. And you know what? It kept the poverty spirit broken. It kept the fear off of us. Now, we didn't spend what we didn't have. But we also weren't afraid to do something important to us just because things were tight. And date night was important. A prosperous soul continues its journey with great joy and confidence in God, all the while ignoring how close "to the ledge" it might be.

It all comes down to personal identity. Either we are held in bondage by or empowered by what we see in the mirror. The good news is that we have a *spiritual* mirror, the "perfect law of liberty" (James 1:25), which is the Word of God. And this new, holy mirror shines on our new nature that is upright, hopeful, and united with God our Father. So if we are united with our Father, then we have full provision for life and abundant supply of finances for all endeavors. We just need to pack our soul with that truth so that no thoughts to the contrary can thrive in us. We must meditate on internal realities rather than external conditions. Rather than using our online bank login to tell us of our possibilities, we let Philippians 4:19 do it, "And my God shall supply all your need according to His riches in glory by Christ Jesus." Confessing scriptures like this, on purpose, over a period of time, expecting revelation knowledge to spring forth in our heart, is how we cause change on the inside of us.

God is our Heavenly Father. He knows what we need, and He will always provide for us. One of the Hebrew names for God is "Jehovah-Jireh", which is translated "The Lord Who provides", and even more literally, "The Lord Who sees and will see to it" (Genesis 22:12-14). Providing for His children is part of God's very nature. We only need to know and believe that. Breaking the poverty mentality requires some heavy thought, some sincere study and declaration of God's Word, and some verbal praise to God about that very fact. When it permeates our heart, we'll detect it and know that we've arrived at our new internal reality.

Remember, money is only a tool. It is to be gained, but only to be used and used properly. As we get our faith wrapped around "unrighteous mammon", we'll soon find that we are lords over money rather than money lording over us with threats, anxieties, and laughter. So put some action to your faith and let this scripture be the final word on the matter for the rest of your life, "And God *is* able to make all grace abound toward you, that you, always having all sufficiency in all things, may have an abundance for every good work" (2 Corinthians 9:8). *All sufficiency in all things* sounds pretty confident doesn't it? Let's plan on that. Just keep in mind the purpose for the abundance is "every good work". So, get to work. Build the Kingdom. Do something beneficial for others. Be productive with what you have. And know that God will do the prospering part.

And again, breaking the poverty mentality includes breaking our *desire for riches*. Desiring something leads to loving it, and we have to be honest with what's in our hearts. "He who loves silver will not be satisfied with silver; Nor he who loves abundance, with increase. This also *is* vanity" (Ecclesiastes 5:10). "For the love of money is a root of all kinds of evil, for which some have strayed from the faith in their greediness, and pierced themselves through with many sorrows. But you, O man of God, flee these things" (1 Timothy 6:10-11). When people lack something, the tendency is to lust after it. Don't let it happen to you. Rather, convince yourself today that you have plenty of money to live and accomplish exactly what's needed for today. Tomorrow is another story, which will always be told according to what's on the inside of you.

Once we get rid of the poverty mentality, the first link in the chain is secured, and we can move to the next.

# PROSPERITY LINK #2
# WORK

Most people do it. Many people dream of not doing it. Some people refuse to do it. And numerous people don't do it very well. What is it? That four letter word called 'work'. But this four letter word is not a bad one, but rather one that we humans were created *for*. I realize that most people are doing it by default anyway. But we need to work *God's way*. The second link to prosperity is a healthy, principled, mentally-stable work life. If we develop the right motives and attitudes about work, get insight into the will of God about working, and let God lead us in our career choices, the grace of God will cause our work life to be a delight. And we can secure another link in the chain of prosperity.

Humans are built to work. It is in our nature. God made us in His image. And God works. Six days He worked to inaugurate this world. Some have incorrectly assumed that walking with God would mean that money miracles would replace our need to work, that they might just quit their job, quote prosperity scriptures all day on the couch, and wait for a money tree to grow in the backyard. It doesn't work that way. God made the earth for mankind and then gave us our command to "subdue the earth". Even when there was only paradise—no sin, no evil, no hardship—mankind still had a job: tend the garden. The only difference after the fall was that the ground was hardened and cursed, mankind was expelled from the garden of Eden, and sweat was added to our work week. But the plan of God for us to work remains. And it will remain forever. Some have the misconception that this life is all about vacations and leisure. But it's not. Vacation time is later. We've got to work while it is day. The night is coming, when no man can work (John 9:4).

Actually, here is our future as a follower of Christ: we have one earth life to live and succeed in with God. Then we go to heaven for a seven year preparation and celebration of our holy wedding with the Lamb and also to prepare for our return. Then we come back to earth with Christ for a thousand years to reign on the earth (that's work). And then heaven and earth are re-done, and we get a brand new holy assignment. So you and I have at least another thousand years to labor with God. Better to figure that out now rather than grumble our way Monday through Friday about how much we dislike working.

The business system of this earth life was created by God. It is an exchange—a trading system—where if I want something, I must either produce it myself or produce something for others who have it. God has made us *individually insufficient*. We need each other. Each of us is to provide something that others need—whether a product, a service, or a piece of information; we all have something to contribute. It's not rocket science, but clearly there are millions of people trying to skirt this simple, God-ordained system of business.

God is so serious about working that He even gives strict instruction to the Church on how to treat those who refuse to work.  It is a dishonor to God and our Church family to not be productive.

> "But we command you, brethren, in the name of our Lord Jesus Christ, that you withdraw from every brother who walks disorderly and not according to the tradition which you have received from us... For even when we were with you, we commanded you this: If anyone will not work, neither shall he eat.  For we hear that there are some who walk among you in a disorderly manner, not working at all, but are busybodies. Now those who are such we command and exhort through our Lord Jesus Christ that they work in quietness and eat their own bread.  And if anyone does not obey our word in this epistle, note that person and do not keep company with him, that he may be ashamed.  Yet do not count him as an enemy, but admonish him as a brother" (2 Thessalonians 3:10).

If they don't work, they don't eat.  God said that.  Many have forgotten that.  Many families let their lazy family member just keep on mooching without any parameters or timetables.  So does the government.  Why is it so disorderly and dishonorable?  Because work is part of maturity.  If children don't grow up, something is distorted and distasteful.  And also because it contradicts God's purpose and plan for all human life.  We are to flourish.  We are to populate earth.  We are to build families.  We are to serve one another.  And we are to build God's Kingdom, build His people, and help the whole world know Him.  God never slumbers (Psalm 121:4).  He is active and purposeful.  So when we are diligent in work, we are conveying His nature and character. Not working is childish, irresponsible, and ungodly.

## REASONS PEOPLE DON'T WORK

(As we discuss this, keep in mind that not all work is for direct income. A stay-at-home mom is certainly working and contributing greatly, so that counts. And those who are retired from full time careers can certainly be doing productive things, whether hobby-type or charity work, helping church and family, starting up a part time business, or volunteering or praying at church. The key component is to be contributing somehow rather than only self-indulging or doing nothing.)

So, why don't some people work? First, it's because they are not healthy. To a healthy man, work is a delight. To a sick man, work is a labor and a burden. But there are two sides to health: natural and spiritual. Physical and mental deficiencies can obviously hinder our ability and our desire to work. But so can spiritual deficiencies. If our faith is not secure—if we are not spiritually fit and serving God, then our desires and lifestyle cannot be trusted. The closer we walk with God, the more clearly we understand His will, and the more energy we get from the Spirit to do His Word. If we're charged with His Spirit, it's almost like we're launched out of bed for daily service. If our priorities are right, work is a challenge that is easy and thrilling to take on.

One of the first things I noticed after my translation into the Kingdom of God in my mid-twenties was that I was happy every day and not just the weekends. Whereas, in my old life, I would look forward to the weekend, or to the next event, or to the next party time for my joy and excitement, I found that in my new life in Christ, I had it every single day. I noticed that I was thrilled to wake up, get out of bed, meet with God, and go do something productive, even on *Mondays*. My spiritual life came first, and out of it flowed a vibrant daily productive work life.

Some people don't work, or don't work much, because they'd rather play. Now, I'm all for the work-hard-play-hard approach to everything. But we must keep the play part in check or it could lead to idolatry, "And do not become idolaters as were some of them. As it is written, The people sat down to eat and drink, and rose up to play" (1 Corinthians 10:7). Notice, idolatry is not just primitive culture gold statue worship, but refers to a misguided disposition of pleasure seeking that can hog our attention and lure us away from serving God and living by principle.

The next reason people don't work is that they are lazy. Laziness brings people to poverty.

> "I went by the field of the lazy man, And by the vineyard of the man devoid of understanding; And there it was, all overgrown with thorns; Its surface was covered with nettles; Its stone wall was broken down. When I saw it, I considered it well; I looked on it and received instruction: A little sleep, a little slumber, A little folding of the hands to rest; So shall your poverty come like a prowler, And your need like an armed man" (Proverbs 24:30-34).

It may seem like chronic laziness has no immediate repercussion, but poverty will come unexpectedly, and financial needs will show up threatening like an "armed man". I spoke with a brother from New Zealand one time who years prior had been out of work for a couple of years and had gradually stopped looking for a job. I was interested to know what was going through his mind during that time and if he had realized what a rut he was in. His response about going back to work, in his heavy New Zealand accent, was, "Can't be bothered." He had formed such a habit of doing nothing and living carelessly that even *thinking* about work was a bother to him. Bad habits are deceptive and destructive. The good news is that he's back on track with a steady job and pursuing a construction degree.

"The way of the lazy man is as a hedge of thorns" (Proverbs 15:19). "The desire of the lazy man kills him, for his hands refuse to labor" (Proverbs 21:25). Laziness will fence us in and stifle the life out of us.

The lazy man is full of excuses, "The lazy man says, "There's a lion outside. I shall be slain in the streets!" (Proverbs 22:13). What is that? That's being scared of nothing. It's just an excuse. Even though there are definite challenges to getting a job and earning money, or definite shortcomings we may have, or a definite history of misfortune, there is no place for excuses. I realize that there are times when tough things happen and a person needs help. We should help. But it doesn't change the principle. And it can't be allowed to turn into an excuse.

Even if it seems like there are zero jobs available, there are some. Let the command to work be your scripture to stand on in faith, and go work somehow. Go shell peas in the country. Sell things online. Go dress up like the statue of liberty and stand on a street corner with an ad sign for a business in the city. Or go buy a case of water bottles, ice them in a cooler, and sell them at an intersection to all the cars as they stop. Here in Houston during the summer, a person could make a full monthly income by buying the waters at about $0.15 each and selling them for $1.00 each. During the winter, sell chocolate bars or energy drinks at the same intersection. Then after you have accumulated some profits, hire a team to do the same thing at other intersections. Simple, smart, and productive in God's system of business. It only requires a commitment to this second prosperity link and just a tad of ingenuity.

Or how about this. Get a bucket of water and a rubber squeegee. Knock on someone's door and offer to wash their outside windows for $5. After your first house is complete, then go next door and tell them you just washed "Mr. Neighbor's" windows, and offer to wash theirs for $20. Then you have a business. It wasn't a lie. You just had to get started. I always thought it was honorable that some guys would come to my house, offering to re-paint my faded house address number on the curb for a small fee of $15 or so. That was a much better use of their God-given time than begging in the streets.

Some might say, "But that's beneath me." Don't be silly. There is no scripture to support that statement. If you need money to pay your rent or feed your family, *nothing* is beneath you. Even if you are educated and highly experienced in some field, if you're not working in that field, you must work elsewhere for a while. I've seen so many people refuse to take a job that wasn't in their field or didn't pay as much as they were accustomed, yet here they were asking for help with their monthly expenses, mooching off friends, family, and church when they could have had a job and income six months ago. There's no excuse. Take the lower paying job until you get the next one.

Here is the final reason why people won't work. Somehow, they've decided that they don't "need" to. People don't "need" to work when they are thieves. They don't "need" to work when government pays, when Mommy pays, when they are good gamblers, when they are fine with begging and mooching, or when they are already rich. A large majority of people are under the assumption that if they had enough money, they wouldn't "need" to work. They are wrong. Nowhere in scripture are we told that work ceases after we have ample money. Think of Abraham. He had great possessions and wealth, but he couldn't just quit in God's plan. God had something for him to do, just like He has for you and I. Think of David and Solomon. They had plenty of money for many lifetimes, yet they both had things to accomplish. There was no retirement from working and producing, for they were God's people. God's people don't quit producing. We are made for it.

And notice this. Because we are designed to add value to society, we are not really happy if we don't do it. It is a most satisfying experience for every man or woman to put in a good hard day's work and then lay down to sleep at night, completely satisfied with his or her accomplishments. If someone goes for long periods of time without being productive, they usually end up depressed, anxious, hopeless, or angry on the inside. Though their feelings can be covered up, deep down they feel useless, without purpose, and unfulfilled. It can happen to teenagers who ought to be getting their first job. It can happen to people who are between jobs. It can happen to retirees. And really, it can happen to anyone whose purpose seems to have faded away from them.

I've noticed something over the past fifteen years and have been inquiring about it for some time now, interviewing parents and young adults when I can. It is this: there seems to be an alarming increase of high school grads who aren't interested in working, aren't interested in any further education after high school, and aren't even interested in getting a driver license so they can drive to some place by themselves. I'm not sure where we've missed it. But I do know that raising up spiritually mature members of Church and society requires the preparation for and pursuit of a successful work life. At some point for everyone, it boils down to making a committed decision to work faithfully and enjoy it.

## MOTIVE

One of the challenges we face in America is to break the common mentality of earning money *so I can one day retire and not work anymore*. Again, there are no scriptures to substantiate that goal. The reason some get so out of order about work and money is that they've missed the real spiritual motive for *why* we work. We don't work for money. We don't work to pay bills. We don't work now so we can stop working later. Instead, we work by principle because it's *right*. We work to have something *to give* to others. We work because money is a *tool* that is needed to create things, grow things, and bless people. We always need a stream of money coming in.

Even if we are able to end our careers at a certain age, or sell our business after many years, or accumulate enough wealth for ten lifetimes for all our family, we'd better not plan on stopping being productive. It's one thing to slow down a bit or take some time to enjoy your earnings. But even in retirement, we need something good to do with our hands and mind. If not, both can be lost. And again, for something to count as work doesn't mean we must be paid money for it. Volunteering at your church counts. Volunteering to help with the grandkids counts. Going to the mall to win souls once a week counts. And any other productive thing can count. Just realize that providing goods or services or love for your fellow man is God's system, and doing good is what we were built for, "For we are His workmanship, created in Christ Jesus for good works, which God prepared beforehand that we should walk in them" (Ephesians 2:10).

We don't work just for ourselves—for "me and my four and no more". Even after we're personally taken care of, we keep working to bless others. "...let him labor, working with his hands what is good, that he may have something to give him who has need" (Ephesians 4:28). We don't just work to "make a living". We work to "make a *giving*". Abraham, the pioneer of God's favor and blessing, wasn't blessed just for himself. God blessed him so that *through him*, "all families of the earth could be blessed" (Genesis 12:3). And so it is with us.

So, even if you've received good severance pay from your *last* job, it doesn't mean you delay looking for your *next* job.

Use the time to get ahead, so by the time you start your next job, your severance savings has increased your wealth. And you also feel better about yourself, because it's right. Even if unemployment is paying well, it is unbefitting to be lazy in your job search. You can't allow yourself to create bad, lethargic habits. Stay productive.

When I first left my career to go into full-time ministry, I really didn't have an established ministry to go into. All I knew was that God informed me it was time to leave my job. So I did. But I also had a plan. And that plan was not to lounge around in my pajamas all day waiting for something to happen. Friday, I left my consulting job. Monday morning I arrived at my church with my suit and tie on, briefcase and Bible in hand, ready to volunteer for whatever was needed. Maybe the suit and tie was a bit much, but that was my routine—show up early and ready. Shortly thereafter, the secretary position opened temporarily, and I was offered the job answering phones. I took it. When she came back after pregnancy, I was offered to stay on as a church worker. That's what I did for the next two years.

When I began to travel and preach, the only office I had was adjacent to my bedroom at home. But when I was in town, it was no time to sleep in like a college kid. I was always up by 7:00 a.m. or so, prayed up, cleaned up, shaved, dressed as if I were going somewhere, and in my office by 8:00 a.m. to study and seek how the Lord would have me help a lost and hurting world. Staying in my morning house clothes all day without showering, shaving, and combing my hair would only prove that I wasn't expecting much to happen in my life. So, even if you're just waiting for some employer call-backs for a job, go ahead and get ready by faith.

The motive is not about becoming rich. "Do not overwork to be rich" (Proverbs 23:4). "Rich" is *not* an effective motive for working hard. Successful entrepreneurs, though they all expect that money will come, aren't doing it only for the money. They do it because they are driven with some idea or talent that they feel they must bring to the world. Bill Gates created the Microsoft oligopoly not because he was trying to make money, but because he was infatuated with the technology of programming computers. Warren Buffet was never in it for the material things he could buy. He lives a very modest life. Rather, he found himself consumed with succeeding in his ability to analyze and buy companies. He just loves what he does and is still doing it in his eighties.

So, don't just start a business. Rather, find a problem and create a solution. Or find out what people need or want, and provide it. Keep the motive focused on the benefit you're supplying to others, and the business will come.

## INTEGRITY

It also matters *how* we work—that we do it uprightly, with excellence, integrity, and humility. We've got to work well even if no one is looking, and even if we don't like our job. So, don't ever violate your conscience in a business deal or on a time card. "Wealth gotten by dishonesty shall be diminished" (Proverbs 13:11). Always be honest and do what's right.

One of our church members testified of a spiritual vision he had, where God took him to heaven to see some wonderful things. At the end of his trip, the Lord was going to speak to him personally, and this is what He said, "Read Ephesians 6:6". *That was it.* Can you believe that? Out of all the things Jesus could have spoken to him, He only quoted this brother a scripture! That's how important God's written Word is to us all. To me, that sounds just like God. Just when we think our problem is so complex that we need a special lengthy conference call with God, all we really need is a scripture. What is Ephesians 6:6? It's the command to do our work as unto the Lord, not being 'men-pleasers', but doing the will of God from our heart. And it changed this brother's life.

And for further witness,

> "Bondservants, obey in all things your masters according to the flesh, not with eyeservice, as men-pleasers, but in sincerity of heart, fearing God. And whatever you do, do it heartily, as to the Lord and not to men, knowing that from the Lord you will receive the reward of the inheritance; for you serve the Lord Christ" (Colossians 3:22-24).

Don't look at your employer or supervisor as the one in charge of your salary, status, or promotion. It is God. "For promotion cometh neither from the east, nor from the west, nor from the south. But God is the Judge: He puts down one, and exalts another" (Psalm 75:6-7). So, don't spend any thought on how you can manipulate yourself into some advantage in the eyes of your supervisor.

And finally, remember that our first Christian calling carries a clear responsibility to the people around us—to be a light and a witness of the gospel of Jesus Christ. Because of that, I'm a firm believer that the first reason for God placing us at a certain job is for the sake of the people there that we can impact. Until we are faithful in our Christian witness at our current job, God doesn't seem very interested in promoting us to another one. If we haven't been a great example of Christ with our *current* group of people, why would God want to send us elsewhere to taint *another* group of people? Again, it's all about living by faith and living by the principles of pleasing God and helping others.

## ALL WORK IS NOT CREATED EQUAL

"They" say that we should all find a job that we enjoy. "Find something you love to do and get paid for it." But I would like to find "them" and have a little chat. You see, when we tell a high school student that, we are doing them a great disservice. Why? Because high school students usually have no idea what they love to do. The majority only like a few things they've found to fill their spare time: video games, sports, music, social media, and goofing off. Most of them really only like "playing". And there are very few good jobs that involve playing. Most students have no idea of real life business and all the jobs that people are paid to do, and that none of those jobs involve frivolous activities. They don't have all the right options laid out for them. How about this: I like fishing and golfing. And so do millions of other people. Does that mean we should all be fishing guides and golf course workers? Hopefully not.

So, what we need to do with teenagers is explain how for the rest of their lives, they will be working forty to fifty hours per week, so they should want to be paid *well* for each of those hours. So, coach them this way, "Find something you have *the grace of God* to do, and do it well!" If you're good in math, head that way. If you're creative, head this way. If you have compassion for people, think about doing this, etc. Kids tend to choose the easiest route before them. They need help to take the *right* route. Like arrows, children must be aimed with purpose, "Like arrows in the hand of a warrior, So are the children of one's youth" (Psalm 127:4).

Not all work is created equal. Some have put in personal education time early, so that for the remainder of their lives, their effort carries more value with it. The more specialized your expertise is, the more someone is willing to pay you for it. There is a tendency among the poor to grudge against the rich with the logic that *I'm sweating harder and working longer for less pay, and that's not fair.* But it *is* fair. When fewer people have the skill to do a certain job, that job pays more. Nothing wrong with flipping hamburgers, but it can be done by almost anyone, so it pays minimum wage. Restaurant manager positions, however, usually have the prerequisite of people skills, financial analysis skills, problem solving skills, and usually a college degree. As a result, they are paid more than the guy slapping cheese on the meat. Everyone sort of knows this or learns this eventually. But it takes faith effort to make education a priority early in life. Even unsaved people are sometimes found using their faith—not faith in God, but they are putting effort into doing that which they believe in—and they are emphasizing education and diligence with their future in mind.

Being great at something is never accidental. Ralph Waldo Emerson said that "Shallow men believe in luck. Strong men believe in *cause and effect*." Someone else once said, "I am a great believer in luck. But what I've found is that the harder I work, the luckier I get".

Work is a delight. It's what we were created for. The call to work carries purpose. It gives *food to the soul*. Jesus said, "My food is to do the will of Him who sent me, and to finish His work" (John 4:34). The call to work gives motivation to get healed, get out of bed, and do something to fulfill the will of God. It pleases Him. And it is the second link in connecting us to real prosperity.

# PROSPERITY LINK #3
# GIVE

In some parts of the world where monkeys are prevalent, one of the ways the indigenous people catch them for food is by using the monkey's own stinginess against them. They hollow out a gourd, or create a cone-shaped cage and attach it to the ground or to a tree, and place either a banana, peanuts, or some other food inside. The hole in the top is cut just large enough for the monkey to squeeze an open hand into, but not large enough for the monkey's closed fist to come out. So, once it grabs the food inside, it is trapped. The obvious solution for the monkey would be to let go of its prized possession, but it won't do it. The monkey's fear of letting go of its treasure has trapped it. The trapper approaches the frantic monkey and easily scoops him up.

The same can happen with God's people. The devil traps people into poverty by their own stinginess. People think, *If I give it, then I won't have it*. But they are wrong. God's way is to give so we can receive—to plant so we can harvest—to sow so we can reap—to be liberal in giving to others so He can be liberal in giving to us. God's supernatural system of giving of our substance transcends natural thinking and living. And it is required for true prosperity. This third link in the chain is all about you and I being generous givers, "He who sows sparingly will also reap sparingly, and he who sows bountifully will also reap bountifully" (2 Corinthians 9:6).

It shouldn't be a big surprise. It seems that almost everything in the Kingdom of God—His system of life and living—is quite the opposite from the world's way. To be first, we've got to be last. To live, we've got to die. To be great, we've got to be a servant. To sit at the front, we've got to start in the back. To be lifted up, we've got to get low. And to receive, we've got to give, "Give, and it will be given to you: good measure, pressed down, shaken together, and running over will be put into your bosom. For with the same measure that you use, it will be measured back to you" (Luke 6:38). In context, that scripture is referring to the way we treat people with forgiveness, love, and mercy will determine what is returned to us. But it also reveals a *general* principle of God—that *whatever* we give we'll receive back with multiplied return. And that includes money.

God is the supplier of our seed. If we keep planting, He'll keep filling our seed sack. "He who supplies seed to the sower, and bread for food, supply and multiply the seed you have sown" (2 Corinthians 9:10). I heard a minister friend of ours, Mark Hankins, say that "If you will get addicted to giving, God will support your habit." And it's true. One year Joni and I gave our really nice Suburban to a church family. Two years later, someone from another state gave us their beautiful luxury motor home and gave us permission to sell it for cash if we wanted. Glory to God. We sold it for four times what our Suburban was worth. R.W. Schambach preached a message all the time, "You can't beat God giving". It's true. God will always out-give you when you do it with a right heart.

*Love* is the nature of God. And that means that *giving* is the nature of God. God's love is not a feeling, but an action. Love desires to satisfy *others* at the expense of self, because *love desires to give*. On the other hand, selfishness desires to satisfy *self* at the expense of others because selfishness is stingy. The entire salvation plan is built on love, which always gives, "For God so loved the world that He *gave*..." When we are born again, something radical takes place on the inside of us. Our nature changes from selfish and greedy to loving and giving. A new desire is birthed in us to bless others. Not everyone yields to that desire. And not everyone fully consecrates their life enough to let the new nature out. But it's in there nonetheless, and we're all called to do it, even when it comes to money.

Before I was devoted to God, my friends and I would haggle over who paid for what—who paid for gas, who didn't ante up at the dinner table, and who was always short, trying to split everything we did fifty-fifty. After I was in the Kingdom, I suddenly didn't care. I'd gladly pay more just to be a blessing. Before I loved God, I never gave any money to the Church. After I loved Him, I suddenly wanted to give *everything* to the Church. That's what the love of God does to a person, "The love of God has been poured out in our hearts by the Holy Spirit who was given to us" (Romans 5:5). Once I was born again and renewed on the inside, I wanted to bless people, both strangers and friends. As exciting as it is to *get* something, it's actually more blessed to give than to receive (Acts 20:35). For people filled with God, giving should be natural.

One reason people don't give is because of fear. They are scared that they won't have enough. Again, love is the answer.  "...perfect love casts out fear, because fear involves torment.  But he who fears has not been made perfect in love" (1 John 4:18).  The closer to love that we are, the less fear we have.  Why is that?  Because God *is* love, so *close to love* means *close to God*.  And *close to God* means *strong faith* and *scared of nothing*.

If your finances ever seem to get stuck, check up on your "giver" and make sure it's not rusted.  If it is, oil it up with some generous giving here and there and watch the windows of Heaven open back up.  Buy someone's groceries in line at the store, buy some school clothes for a family at church, give some cash to a stranger God leads you to, or on a different level, give a car away.  Whatever it takes, we can't get rusty.

Another reason people don't give, in particular to God, is because they place little value on the Kingdom of God. They have no desire to give at church because the theoretical value they may profess to place on God doesn't translate to actual desire for the things of God.  The truth is that we are usually willing to pay for, or put money in, anything that we value.  We value our home and car, so we spend money on them.  We value our children, so no problem spending our last dime on them.  We value our electronics and our restaurant meals, so there goes more.  We don't have any problem giving money to Apple, because it gives us the iPhone.  And we have no problem with supporting Outback Steakhouse, because it gives us the Bloomin' Onion.  One of our church leaders remembers her momma's proverb, "You have money for what you want to have money for."  And it's true.

What about God?  What about the gospel ministry we receive at church?  How much is it worth to us?  When "worth-y is the Lord" rings true in our soul, it's easy to give our money to Him. Salvation is free. But afterward, we see the value of this salvation and rejoice in giving for Kingdom and Church growth.

One time in a certain church revival during offering time, I was contemplating if I really needed to give something or not. I normally always gave cheerfully, but these meetings had been going on every night for several weeks, and I had been giving faithfully every night. So, in my mind, the words kept coming, "You don't need to give any more. You've already given enough." But I recognized that voice. It was the *devil*. Or, it could have just been my carnal nature speaking up—I really don't care which. But when I recognized it, I laughed and thought, *That's it—I'm giving all I have on me. No devil is going to doubt me into not giving.* So I reached into my wallet, maybe hoping for only a few bucks to be there, but there were four $20 bills. I cheerfully tossed my $80 into the bucket as it passed and rejoiced in my heart, knowing I had "broke the devil's back", even though it meant my net worth had decreased. After the meeting was over, a guy walked over to me and shook my hand. But something was scratching my hand, as there was a piece of paper in his. *A Pentecostal handshake*, I thought. (That's what people have called it, referring to when the spirit of generous giving gets on someone. And as it turns out, it seems to happen more among the Spirit-filled Christians than the non, hence "Pentecostal". But it sure makes life fun!) Well, when that happened, I did what most people do. I casually *ran outside as fast as I could* to see what it was. I got into my truck and opened my hand. It was a check for $1,000. Glory to God—I knew I had done something spiritual, and God had blessed. (By the way, *giving* is another powerful way to break the poverty mentality off of us, get the devil off our shoulder, and prove to the unseen world that we mean business in our covenant with God.)

## TO WHOM ARE WE GIVING?

Giving is a very personal act of faith between us and God. We are giving to *Him*. Though the money ends up in a bank account and is spent on earthly things, the actual act of giving is toward Him. In the Old Testament, it was the Levitical high priests who received the offerings for the work of God. Now, we have no earthly high priest to do that. New Testament pastors have not replaced Old Testament priests. Rather, Jesus is now our High Priest (Hebrews 3:1, 4:14). He presented the sacrifice of blood on the altar. He is the receiver of all offerings, of all tithes, of all monetary giving. So, anything given in the name of Jesus is seen by Him and received by Him (Mark 12:41). Regardless of how effectively that money is used, it is holy. The act of faith was holy, and the blessing of it is holy.

## HOW MUCH ARE WE SUPPOSED TO GIVE?

But still, how much does God expect us to give? There has been much debate on whether or not the "tithe" command is still in effect. *Tithe* is not a religious term, but a math term. It simply means *one-tenth*, and therefore, one-tenth of income. Does God require that we give one-tenth of our income to the Church in order to avoid the curse or keep the windows of heaven open upon us? If we only have Malachi 3, then it certainly appears so,

> "Will a man rob God? Yet you have robbed Me! But you say, 'In what way have we robbed You?' In tithes and offerings. You are cursed with a curse, for you have robbed Me, even this whole nation. Bring all the tithes into the storehouse, that there may be food in My house, and try Me now in this, says the Lord of hosts, if I will not open for you the windows of heaven and pour out for you such blessing that there will not be room enough to receive it" (Malachi 3:8-10).

However, this brings us to a very important theological pivot point about the two parts of the Bible—the Old Testament and New Testament. The Old Testament (Covenant) was God's original agreement with mankind through Abraham. But out of that Old Covenant sprang a New Covenant that is called "a better covenant" with "better promises" (Hebrews 8:6), which is anchored in the cross of Jesus Christ and which replaced that Old Covenant and made it obsolete (Hebrews 8:13). Now, our rule of Bible interpretation allows us to discard certain aspects of the Old Testament but keep others. If a certain principle or blessing passes through to the New Testament, it is valid. But many things didn't—particularly the curse part, "Christ has redeemed us from the curse of the law, being made a curse for us" (Galatians 3:13). So, when Malachi, under the Old Testament, said people were cursed for robbing God, he didn't mean us—believers in Christ. He only meant people who were under the law. And we're not under the law, but under grace (Romans 6:14, Galatians 5:4). Under the law, the curse was God's decided penalty for an act of disobedience. So, if we are redeemed from that curse, then we are exempt from that penalty. For those who are in Christ, there is no penalty from God for disobedience. Jesus took our punishment for sin. We're exempt from the curse because of the cross of Jesus Christ, and that applies to the curse for holding back tithes and offerings. And that's why so many disobedient believers in God are still alive and partially happy.

So, to really understand giving to God, we can't look to the law of Moses and the prophets. We must go back further than the law and look deeper to find principles that can carry through to the New Testament. You see, most everything religious seems a lot easier if we just have some natural, carnal rules to follow, "Just tell me what I gotta do, and I'll do that to please God just enough." But one plan and purpose of God was to put His Holy Spirit in us so we would do right things without being forced. He removed the law from us as our schoolmaster (tutor), and wrote the command of love in our heart, "Wherefore the law was our schoolmaster to bring us unto Christ, that we might be justified by faith. But after that faith is come, we are no longer under a schoolmaster" (Galatians 3:24-25 KJV). Now, we must do things spiritually, from our heart and by following the Holy Spirit. And that is a bit more difficult because it's not as clear and definite to our physical senses. Now, we give money for God's purposes by *principle*, simply because it's right and wonderful and not because we're forced.

*Principled giving* is how it all began anyway with men of God who knew what was right. The rule of law did not start it. It was done long before a law was ever needed. Abraham decided to give one-tenth of his earnings, not because he was told to, but just because it felt right to honor God (Genesis 14:20). He gave it to the high priest at the time, Melchizedek, in response to Melchizedek doing one thing: he blessed Abraham. Now, Jesus is our current High Priest (rather than a man—Hebrews 7). And it is Him we are giving to in response to His blessing *us*.

Even before Abraham, there was Abel. Abel shows an even deeper principle than that of an offering *amount*. If you recall, Cain and Abel brought offerings to God without being told to do so. However, God "had respect unto" Abel's offering but not Cain's. This is what made Cain so mad that he killed his brother. But we must ask the question, why did God not accept Cain's offering? It's in the scripture,

> "It came to pass that Cain brought an offering of the fruit of the ground to the Lord. But He did not respect Cain and his offering. And Cain was very angry, and his countenance fell. Abel also brought of the firstborn of his flock and of their fat. And the Lord respected Abel and his offering" (Genesis 4:3-5).

If we notice the exact language, that Cain brought "*an* offering", but Abel brought "of the *firstborn* of his flock", we see the reason. It is that Abel gave that which was most precious, the firstborn of his flocks, but Cain didn't. Cain should have given his *firstfruits*.

But why would God care, since He hadn't commanded either in the first place? Both guys just did it willingly, it seemed. But that's where God knows something that we can't see from the outside. God looks upon the hearts. And when a person doesn't give that which is most precious, most vital, most loved, most important in their own lives to God, it reveals that their heart is not fully toward God. And that's when God isn't touched by their offering. Solomon recognized that principle in Proverbs, "Honor the Lord with your possessions, And with the *firstfruits* of all your increase; So your barns will be filled with plenty, And your vats will overflow with new wine" (Proverbs 3:9-10).

The firstfruits, or the firstborn, is that which we esteem the most. It has to matter to us. So, a little "tip" off the back end doesn't count. Think of it this way: a farmer decides to plant a crop. He tills the ground. His whole family and all his workers get involved in the process. He plants the seed. He waters and waits and waits and waters. The precious fruit begins to show and grow. The whole family yearns with anticipation for three to four months. Finally the fruit begins to ripen and it's time for harvest. Labor increases. Sweat is plentiful. Hard work for the first day is done. And here come the baskets of harvest. The family's mouth is salivating, and their belly is leaping for joy. All the servants are called in from the field to rejoice in the harvest.

Shall they gobble it all up? Not if God is first in their life. When we acknowledge God as our Source and our Provider, we willingly give these firstfruits to Him. I'm not saying that everyone should be bringing fruits and veggies to the church offering, but rather that this is how we must feel when our paycheck arrives. The first, best, most yearned for portion should go to God. Not the leftovers. Not just anything. Not just a couple of crumbs. But the first, substantial, healthy part. Why? Because He is first and favorite in our lives. And so is all of His Kingdom stuff—the Church, the ministers, and the gospel spreading.

So, how much is the *firstfruits*? It's the amount that begins to matter to you—the amount that touches your heart. Is it 10 percent? I would say usually *at least*. Why is it that when people argue about not giving 10 percent, they never want to give *more* than 10 percent, but always *less*? By principle, 10 percent seems like a good place to start. But why not go for 11 percent at some point? Or 20 percent sometimes? Why not increase your love for God's Kingdom and increase your giving proportionately? Or is it possible to love God and have your heart totally consecrated to God without giving of your substance to Him?

Definitely not. Jesus said, "For where your treasure is, there your heart will be also" (Luke 12:34). If you want your heart to truly be with God, you'll need to give your treasure to God. This has nothing to do with paying for your salvation or earning a blessing, for we are saved and blessed by faith alone even if we are stingy in life. But it does reveal a spiritual reality that gives evidence of where our heart really is. We all know that money is one of our treasures, and that we all need it to live well on the earth. So a person who doesn't put a good portion of their money into the Kingdom will never be Kingdom-minded. If a person doesn't give money for the spreading of the gospel, they'll never care much about the gospel. And likewise, if a person doesn't give money to their local church, they'll not care about their local church. If you want to see yourself attend church more faithfully, start giving at least one-tenth to your home church. Your heart will follow your money. You'll even start caring that your church grows and is healthy. It is very clear. I've noticed that some people, deep in their heart, know that. They know that if they start giving money to a church, they'll start feeling responsible to be there and obligated to walk with God. But because they are sometimes not willing to really consecrate their life to Him fully, they restrain themselves and continue a giving*less*, unfaithful spiritual life so that they can keep their free time on Sundays and their money, too. The tithe is called *holy*. It is holy because it represents the supremely sacred part of a person's life—our heart. And when our heart is right, our faith is secure. And that allows God to move in our life.

## GIVING BY FAITH, NOT BY LAW

For a long time, churches didn't understand this, so they more or less coerced people to give by law and threat of curse. But now under the New Testament, we are commanded to *not* give out of coercion, "So let each one give as he purposes in his heart, not grudgingly or of necessity; for God loves a cheerful giver" (2 Corinthians 9:7). Now, we give not because *we have to*, but because *we want to*. At our church we teach that if you don't want to, then don't. Our motive for giving must be faith and trust. We must believe right about why and how much. And we must be happy and cheerful about it. If we can't give in faith, believing that it's right and good, then it would actually be a sin if we did it, "...whatever is not from faith is sin" (Romans 14:23). I've noticed that there are many Christians who have been giving somewhat grudgingly, trying to please God but not really wanting to part with their money. And it's put them in a bad place spiritually and with no financial benefit. (Now, don't get me wrong here. I certainly believe we should be giving to God. But if we refuse for some reason, then we should learn some truth about it so we can get some faith for it. And then do it once we believe it.)

I grew up with faithful parents who always gave a tenth to God. I knew it was a right thing to do. I planned that one day when I was an adult, I would do the same. (I didn't realize I could have done the right thing even as a child and as an adolescent. I guess I thought small amounts were insignificant.) And I had fallen into the trap of many who put it off until circumstances get perfect, "He that observes the wind will not sow; and he that regards the clouds will not reap" (Ecclesiastes 11:4). But my plan was that after I graduated college, I would start giving a tenth to God. I didn't. I got my first good-paying job, but somehow forgot about giving to God. I bought a truck. I bought a boat. I spent money on many things. But I kept putting off giving to God. At the time, I wasn't living for God at all, so I was not hearing the truth preached at all. But deep down, I knew that I was neglecting something (many things, actually). One day in my mid-twenties, I was watching television and saw the 700 Club was doing a telethon. My family had always appreciated and trusted Pat Robertson and his television ministry, so I trusted him. I decided to pledge some money—$100 a month. It wasn't really a full tenth, but it meant a lot to *me*, and I began giving faithfully. My life still appeared quite "heathen", but behind closed doors, I was honoring God. I had no idea what I had done. I had no idea of the spiritual significance and the new road I had put myself on. I had no idea I had put my heart in God's hands by giving money to a gospel preacher. And I had no idea that within one year, I'd be repented, baptized, delivered from darkness, and sold out to God. But I was. And in hindsight, I realize that pledging my treasure to God opened the door of my heart.

I've never seen a spiritually healthy Christian who wasn't consistently giving a good portion of their income to God. It just doesn't happen. Our giving is largely a reflection of our spirituality. Those who "touch" the tithes and firstfruits (by spending them) usually watch their finances go haywire and end up in a vicious cycle of not giving, then not having enough to give, then not giving, and so on. Why do they go haywire? Because when we're not trusting God, we open the door to the devil.

Even for those who've been faithfully giving a tenth for a while, be careful not to get complacent and dry in your giving. Remember, our faith should always be increasing, so the tithe is not the end goal. Offerings on top of the tithe are necessary to keep us free. Or why not break out from tithing on what we make, and rather tithe on what we want to make before we're making it? That's faith.

There is great freedom in being able to give money to God in faith. It causes us to trust Him. It reminds us the windows of heaven are open, so our confidence remains secure. It keeps us from being stingy. It keeps our heart clean and powerful. It disconnects us from serving unrighteous mammon (material things), "No servant can serve two masters; for either he will hate the one and love the other, or else he will be loyal to the one and despise the other. You cannot serve God and mammon" (Luke 16:13).

The more we give to God, the less we have for worthless pleasures or sinful indulgences. The annual $5,000 or so that heathen Chas was no longer spending on heathen things quickly found its way into the Kingdom, as it should. And the cleaner our heart is, the stronger our faith is.

Some are too focused on comparing amounts. They look at the rich people of the church and compare their smaller gift, concluding that theirs doesn't do as much, so why worry with it. Just let the rich support the church and its projects since the poor among us need every drop they can find. But they are wrong. It's not about the amount. It's about how much the amount means to the person giving it. And it's about the sum of every part making God's unique Church design fully functional. Remember the poor widow woman who gave all she had?

> "Now Jesus sat opposite the treasury and saw *how* the people put money into the treasury. And many who were rich put in much. Then one poor widow came and threw in two mites which make a quadrans. So He called His disciples to Himself and said to them, Assuredly, I say to you that this poor widow has put in more than all those who have given to the treasury; for they all put in out of their abundance, but she out of her poverty put in all that she had, her whole livelihood" (Mark 12:41-44).

Notice that Jesus didn't respond with a poverty mindset and tell her to keep it since she was poor. Nor did He say her amount was insignificant. He said she actually *put in more* than the rich ones. He responded with spiritual insight, knowing that God would return it back to this woman, with good measure, pressed down, shaken together, and running over. The motivation behind our gift is more important than the gift itself, "And though I bestow all my goods to feed the poor...but have not love, it profits me nothing" (1 Corinthians 13:3). If our heart is not right, even a large gift doesn't count. So, if a rich person was able to give a huge gift, larger than everyone else combined, it wouldn't even register in heaven unless the amount truly meant something to the person who gave it.

God isn't after our money. He is after our heart. He wants our whole life. But if He doesn't have the money part of our life, He's missing a huge part of it. Remember the rich young ruler who came to discuss with Jesus how to gain eternal life? After professing that he'd been keeping the commands, Jesus touched on something deeper.

> "Then Jesus, looking at him, loved him, and said to him, "One thing you lack: Go your way, sell whatever you have and give to the poor, and you will have treasure in heaven; and come, take up the cross, and follow Me. But he was sad at this word, and went away sorrowful, for he had great possessions" (Mark 10:21-22).

Out of love, Jesus was trying to help the man part with the thing keeping him from God. The man was trying to serve God, but deep down, his heart was too attached to mammon. It happens to Christians all the time. They believe in Jesus, but they can't follow Him faithfully and powerfully because they won't part with their money.

And notice this: Jesus told him to get rid of *all* his money, not just a tenth. So, if we really want to argue about doing away with the tenth completely, then we'll need to open up to New Testament giving, where giving *all* is a possibility. Hopefully, every one of us has had that true discipleship moment of either giving *all* of our money to God or at least being *willing* to give it all if He asked for it. It is written that the early Church did it a couple times,

> "Now all who believed were together, and had all things in common, and sold their possessions and goods, and divided them among all, as anyone had need. So continuing daily with one accord in the temple, and breaking bread from house to house, they ate their food with gladness and simplicity of heart" (Acts 2:44-46, Acts 4:32).

Of course, we can't *always* give *all*, or we'd never be able to make a purchase or save any money. But the freedom, joy, and willingness to do it should be in us.

Notice this scripture,

> "The light of the body is the eye: if therefore thine eye be single, thy whole body shall be full of light. But if thine eye be evil, thy whole body shall be full of darkness. If therefore the light that is in thee be darkness, how great is that darkness" (Matthew 6:22-23, KJV).

The reference is a little foreign to us, and at first glance it appears to be talking about good and evil. But technically, it's in Matthew 6, which is in the context of money. And it is referring to our spirit of giving. The term *single eye* is a peculiar term to most of us, but overseas, it's used to describe 'a giving person'. I had a friend who had gone to Africa, and he noticed a billboard that read, *Have a Single Eye... Toward the United Way.* It was a *fundraising* advertisement. Either we are a generous "single eyed" person, or we are a stingy "evil eyed" person. True light will shine in our life when we are givers. But if not, Jesus said our whole body will be in darkness.

## A GOOD FARMER NEVER EATS IT ALL

Giving to God doesn't earn us anything in the form of being paid for our act, but there is certainly a great financial blessing in it. Since "The Kingdom of God is as if a man should scatter seed on the ground..." (Mark 4:26), then the principle of seedtime and harvest works in our monetary giving. If we plant seed, we get harvest from it, "Do not be deceived, God is not mocked; for whatever a man sows, that he will also reap" (Galatians 6:7). If we are consistent givers, then we will have consistent harvest. If we skip a season of giving, we are, in essence, scheduling a season of lack sometime in our future. It's very spiritual and very real.

We must be cognizant of this spiritual principle. Far too many times we allow the argument to linger in our minds, *I need this money to live on, so I can't give it.* No good farmer would do that. No farmer would ever eat all his seed, no matter how hungry he was, for he knows that if he doesn't reserve some of his best seed for planting, he will surely starve next year. Think about it. This is not a zero sum game. One corn kernel planted does not equal one corn kernel of harvest. Rather, one corn kernel produces an entire stalk with several ears of corn, each containing about 800 more kernels! Again, though, a poverty mentality is oblivious to spiritual truth like this. Once we grasp it, we'll not just pray for harvest, but we'll start sowing seed for harvest. Farmers could pray all season, but if they didn't plant any seed, they'd be starving...just like Christians who are sporadic in their giving sometimes are.

So, here is the sum of the matter. Our lifestyle of giving is not a law. It is a principle. And it's an obvious link in the chain connecting us to God's prosperity. We give because we love God, we love the Church (Jesus Christ's Body), we love the spreading of the gospel, we love ministers who have dedicated themselves to it, and we love people. We give to the Church, we give to the poor, and we give to others. If we do it in faith, the seed is good. If we do it with right motives, our heart is healthy. And since our heart is the ground that the seed is planted in (the Kingdom of God is within you), then the harvest fields will keep growing. It's not the amount of money given that counts. It's the value our heart places on it and the cheerfulness and faithfulness in which we give it.

# PROSPERITY LINK #4
# DO NOT WORRY

Don't worry about money. Don't worry about bills. Don't over-think your financial circumstances. If you can get a firm handle on this one, you'll secure what tends to be most people's biggest broken prosperity link of all. And if you can't, then all the other links in the chain lose their strength and it will feel like your financial truck is still stuck in the mud.

Just when we think we've got a lot of things going right in the money realm, there's that subtle, nagging, persistent scratch of worry. And it must be exposed and eliminated. To *not worry* is a command of God. Throughout the Bible, God reminds His people to not worry, to not fear, and to not be dismayed. Why is that? Because if I'm worried, I'm not really trusting God. If I'm anxious about a matter, it means I really don't have faith toward God in the matter. And only worry-free faith can connect us to God's hand of prosperity. Worry and faith cannot coexist.

Jesus addressed this in "Christianity 101 – The Sermon on the Mount". This basic finance chapter for believers is very clear, and it should be thought on, rehearsed, and planted firmly in every believer's heart, for it is the foundation of all prosperity from God. At our church, any time someone comes for help with financial challenges, this is my first instruction. If they can't secure this truth in their heart, no praying or counseling is ever going to help.

> "Therefore I say to you, do not worry about your life, what you will eat or what you will drink; nor about your body, what you will put on. Is not life more than food and the body more than clothing? Look at the birds of the air, for they neither sow nor reap nor gather into barns; yet your Heavenly Father feeds them. Are you not of more value than they? Which of you by worrying can add one cubit to his stature? So why do you worry about clothing? Consider the lilies of the field, how they grow: they neither toil nor spin; and yet I say to you that even Solomon in all his glory was not arrayed like one of these. Now if God so clothes the grass of the field, which today is, and tomorrow is thrown into the oven, will He not much more clothe you, O you of little faith? Therefore do not worry, saying, 'What shall we eat?' or 'What shall we drink?' or 'What shall we wear?' For after all these things the Gentiles seek. For your Heavenly Father knows that you need all these things. But seek first the Kingdom of God and His righteousness, and all these things shall be added to you" (Matthew 6:25-33).

Jesus gets right down to the basics of life and commands us not to worry about our necessities. If we want all things taken care of, we're required not to worry. Worrying sets us back. He even connects the personal title of "O you of little faith" to the person who worries. And no Christian wants to be called *that*. He says we humans are better than birds and flowers—that if God feeds birds who don't even have to get a job, and if God clothes the flowers who do absolutely nothing but grow around looking pretty, how much more will He care for you and I (His actual children, who actually *do* get jobs and work hard)?  If we find ourselves worrying about money, we might as well stick a little name badge on our shirts that reads, "O Me of Little Faith".  Ouch!

This is basic trust in our Father.  Consider the best earthly parents you can think of—how well they care for their children and provide constant, wonderful provision for them, including food, spending money, and even gifts to make them happy.  God is way better than that.  Our Heavenly Father is better than even the best earthly parent, "If you then, being evil, know how to give good gifts to your children, how much more will your Father who is in heaven give good things to those who ask Him" (Matthew 7:11).  So why are we worried, O we of little faith?

That is supposed to settle it.

Jesus mentions that the *Gentiles* are seeking those basic necessities of life, implying that we should do the opposite. What does He mean?  He is highlighting the fact that people without a covenant and without God are all worried about these basic life essentials.  So, why would *we* be like *them*?

I'll tell you why.  We only worry because we haven't put proper emphasis on believing this Bible chapter.

Jesus said don't even take any thought about it.  And especially don't take any thought *saying*—saying something dumb and doubtful out of our mouths.  People pray in faith in one moment, but then turn right around and say something in the house that reveals their doubt and double-mindedness, "Well I sure hope I can keep my job" or "I just don't know what we're gonna do…". That stuff should never come out of our mouths!

The worry war is inside of us. It is in our minds. It is really just a form of fear. We could even recognize it as 'uneasiness', where we just have that disturbing feeling in our stomach. I encountered this war early in my walk with God. I had just made a three-month long, prayerful decision in the will of God that it was time to leave my successful career as a business consultant to pursue God's call to me for gospel ministry. And wouldn't you know it. The very next morning after I gave my two-week notice, I woke up paralyzed with fear and anxiety. I had gone to bed extremely happy and excited about being in the will of God, but I woke up oddly stricken with panic. My mind was paralyzed with the thought that I had just made the biggest mistake of my life. The thoughts consumed me. *What have I done? I've just given up all my income and my financial future that I had worked so hard to establish. And I have no job. No ministry. No income. No nothing. What a dummy.* And then down in my heart, God's truth would rise up. I began to think on Matthew 6, Philippians 4:19, and other scriptures where God said that if a man preaches the gospel the gospel will take care of paying him, where God said that providing for His people is part of the covenant, and so on. And the battle raged for about thirty minutes. After thirty minutes of lying almost physically stunned in bed, but combating those thoughts by thinking on and saying God's words, the battle ended. The fear disappeared completely. Then I rose for the day full of joy, and freely served God all day. Until the next morning, when there it was again. Fear showed up, and the whole thing started all over. For thirty minutes. And I won again. This went on for three weeks—every morning—same battle. And every morning I would win and rise with grace and confidence. And then finally it was over. I beat the worry. I won the battle of the mind concerning money and God's promised financial provision. And I can say with all honesty that more than seventeen years have passed and I have never once lost any ground to worrying about money. God has always met my needs, whether little or great, and that silly little demon of fear has rarely come around to fight again. And when it does, I always get on top of it quickly and get my trust back over on God. All glory to the name of Jesus.

(I recall one particular brief moment of about sixty seconds where I was tempted to worry. It was after I asked Joni to marry me, and I suddenly realized that my lean, bachelor style, sleep-in-the-Suburban-on-the-road-when-necessary lifestyle, was about to be replaced with a house mortgage, some elegant "necessities", and Joni leaving her own CPA career soon to answer her own call and join me in full time ministry. Time to panic? Then I caught myself and thought, *Wait a second. God has always taken care of me, and I know He'll do it again somehow.* I cast off the care, and the threat of worry left immediately. It has never returned. And God has always supplied more than enough, both miraculously and consistently for all these years. In both our personal life and also ministry endeavors, we've never missed one bill nor one desire.)

If we'll do our part, God will see that the devil and his anxious thoughts leave us. "Submit to God. Resist the devil and he will flee from you" (James 4:7). It is a spiritual law. If we resist the devil the way that Jesus did, he will leave us. If we don't resist, then we'll have to live with what he gives us.

How did Jesus resist the devil? Three times, Jesus retaliated against Satan's temptation with "It is written...", and then quoted a truth from Scripture. If the devil "punches" with a doubt or temptation, we punch back with a Scripture or a rebuke. It's that simple. And notice this. Not once did I get out of bed during those three weeks until I convinced myself the Word of God was true and that God would do it. Don't ever let the devil get the last punch in. If he punches with a fear tactic, you punch back with the truth. Again. And again. And again. Until you know you've gotten the last word in and it's over. Then carry on with your day. The winner of a fight is always the one who punches last, so never leave a battle with the devil until the last one is you.

The devil's delight is to tempt us with thoughts, suggestions, and wrong reasoning, attempting to get us out of faith and into worry and sin. The strongholds are in our thinking. That's why God tells us that

> **"The weapons of our warfare are not carnal but mighty in God for pulling down strongholds, casting down arguments and every high thing that exalts itself against the knowledge of God, bringing every thought into captivity to the obedience of Christ"** (2 Corinthians 10:4-5).

The devil is after our thought life, and that is where we combat Satan's thoughts with God's thoughts, just as Jesus did. What we think on gets in our heart. And what we say from our heart activates the unseen realm. The moment our mouth speaks, we either trigger the power of life or the power of death (Proverbs 18:21).

How many times has someone told you, "Don't worry, it will be all right"? If there's no explanation behind it, it doesn't have the strength to really help, does it?  Just telling someone to "be positive", and then expect mind-over-matter-will-power to do the job, doesn't work.   However, if the Bible says it, then God says it.  And that means we can bank on it.  "Be anxious for nothing...let your requests be made known to God...and the peace of God...will keep your hearts and minds..." (Philippians 4:6-7).

But there's more.  And it comes from a certain aspect of the cross of Jesus Christ that many people have never known. The prophet Isaiah saw it in the Spirit.  He prophesied what would happen at the Cross long before it happened.  And what did he see?  He saw that the Son of God would redeem the human race by substituting Himself for our punishment. He saw that our immorality would be placed on the Messiah, "the Lord has laid on Him the iniquity of us all" (Isaiah 53:6).  But he saw something else.  It was not just sins and immoralities that Jesus took upon Himself.  "Surely He has borne our griefs and carried our sorrows... He *was* wounded for our transgressions, *He was* bruised for our iniquities; The chastisement for our peace *was* upon Him, And by His stripes we are healed" (Isaiah 53:4-5).  Jesus also took our griefs and sorrows and secured our peace and our healing. But if we look deeper into the meaning of the Hebrew word for 'grief' (Heb. 'choliy'), we see a more complete picture.  In our culture, the word 'grief' is used somewhat limitedly to grieving over a lost loved one or experiencing emotional pain. But in the Hebrew language, 'choliy' has a broader meaning and refers to *calamity, disease, weakness*, and *anxiety*.  Did you see that?  At the Cross, not only did Jesus bare our diseases. He also bore our *anxieties*!  So, just as we have faith that our sins are forgiven and that we are constantly made clean, and just as we can have faith that we are healed from disease, we can also have faith to be delivered from anxiety and worry.

Our covenant with God includes forgiveness of sins, healing of the body, and freedom from anxiety. Some have said that only spiritual healing was secured at the cross. But that is not true. The Cross covered spirit, soul, *and* body. The Apostle Matthew wrote, "And He cast out the spirits with a word, and healed all who were sick, that it might be fulfilled which was spoken by Isaiah the prophet, saying: He Himself took our infirmities and bore our sicknesses" (Matthew 8:17). And then we have even further substitution for poverty and destruction, "For you know the grace of our Lord Jesus Christ, that though He was rich, yet for your sakes He became poor, that you through His poverty might become rich" (2 Corinthians 8:9).

We call it the *great exchange.* He took our place, so we could take His. He was made to be sin, He took on infirmities, sicknesses, and anxieties, and He was made poor—all so we could have the opposite. Jesus took it all! Our part is to believe it, accept it, renew our mind to it, and expect it with full assurance of faith. Christ redeemed us from the curse of the law. To redeem means 'to set free by the payment of a price'. Christ has redeemed us from spiritual death. He has redeemed from the curse of sickness and distress. And He has redeemed us from the curse of poverty. If you want to see detailed proof on what the curse was all about and what we have escaped because of Jesus, read Deuteronomy 28:15-68, and then rejoice about your redemption!

Our covenant was ratified. Our side of the covenant was fulfilled in Christ. Our covenant is in Christ, and our redemption from sin, disease, *and anxiety* was finished when Jesus said it was.   Just believe that.   Don't worry.   And connect to this elusive prosperity link through the finished work of the cross of Jesus Christ.

# PROSPERITY LINK #5
# SAVE AND INVEST

Get rich quick schemes are not Biblical. Saving and investing is. If we want to prosper God's way, saving and investing money on a consistent basis is part of it. Without accumulation, there is no real wealth or monetary strength. So without this link in the prosperity chain, people's financial efforts are like a mouse on a wheel—spinning hard but never going anywhere, waiting for some miracle surprise windfall to come their way. But it never does, because that's not God's system for prosperity.

"Wealth from get-rich-quick schemes quickly disappears; wealth from hard work grows over time" (Proverbs 13:11 NLT). "Wealth gained hastily will dwindle, but whoever gathers little by little will increase it" (Proverbs 13:11 ESV). Notice the words *grows over time* and *little by little*. Most Christians have probably not heard the saving and investing principle preached much. It's not extremely popular in pulpits, as it's not very spectacular nor testimonial, at least not until many years later. But it's very powerful. And it's God's way. It doesn't mean we sacrifice the link of *Giving* to do it, since all links in the chain are essential. But if done by principle, it will ensure prosperity for the individual, and subsequently, the Kingdom. What is *not* God's way is to be lured into a false confidence about the "great wealth transfer" that many Christians are counting on.

The scripture, "...the wealth of the sinner is laid up for the just" (Proverbs 13:22), is referring primarily to the millennial reign of Christ when the "gates shall be open continually...that men may bring to you the wealth of the Gentiles" (Isaiah 60:11, 5).    It is not referring to some cataclysmic economic disruption where the heathen empty their bank accounts for us, but rather a promise that if we need money, it's available if we can believe.    And truly, if we're talking about money for the Kingdom, the best way for a sinner's money to make it into Church is for a sinner to be saved.

In the 'parable of the talents', Jesus called the unfaithful servant "wicked and lazy" for not investing what he had.    If we recall, the particular lord had given three guys different amounts of money for them to use to produce something. The first two used their money to do business and double it. But the third guy went and hid his in the ground out of fear of losing it.    To the first two, their lord congratulated them, but to the third, he rebuked him.

> "His lord said to him, Well done, good and faithful servant; you were faithful over a few things, I will make you ruler over many things. Enter into the joy of your lord. But to the third he said, you wicked and lazy servant...you ought to have deposited my money with the bankers, and at my coming I would have received back my own with interest. Therefore take the talent from him, and give it to him who has ten talents. For to everyone who has, more will be given, and he will have abundance; but from him who does not have, even what he has will be taken away" (Matthew 25:14-29).

Notice that God expects us to use what we have to produce, to trade, to build, and to benefit—with increase. And for any money not used to produce income directly, funnel it to the bankers so it can grow. (By the way, banking, lending, and borrowing are not sins, and neither is investing.) And finally, notice that because the poorest man was unfaithful, wicked, and lazy, the man's lord took what he *did* have and gave it to the richest guy. That's why the rich get richer and the poor get poorer. The rich are faithful to do something worthwhile with their money, and the poor aren't. It's no mystery—God is not interested in giving a person more of anything if they aren't faithful with the little they start with.

Being "good and faithful" applies to everything in life, including *faithful to save and invest.*

In Deuteronomy, when the blessings and curses were detailed, one of the blessings was that, "God will command the blessing on you in your storehouses..." (Deuteronomy 28:8). The question for ourselves is, *Do we have any storehouses?* Notice that *storehouses* is plural. God is a filler and an over-flower. We just need to give Him a place to do it. God is a producer. He likes things fruitful and plentiful. He created the earth, put man in it, and said, "Fill it." Peter gave Him a net, and He filled it. Jesus gave Him a couple fish and loaves, and He filled thousands of bellies and baskets. God is a supplier and a blesser of whatever good faith project we give Him.

So what does it mean for us? First, we ought to have a checking account. And a savings account. And then an investment account. And then a second and third investment account. Whatever we give God to fill, He will fill, good measure, pressed down, shaken together, and running over. The problem is that many believers aren't really believing. They're not believing and expecting God to do anything, and that's why so few Christians have even a savings account, much less an investment account.

I regretfully admit that I was once in that same group. Though I believed greatly in saving and investing, and though my wife and I had several personal storehouses, even after our third year of the church, we still had no church savings account. We had a church checking account, but that was all. In my mind, I was under the mistaken impression that we didn't really need a savings account until we had excess in the checking account. So we kept delaying. And guess what? Our savings never grew because we really had no place for it to accumulate, and we had no plan for it. But one day we were introduced to *The Storehouse Principle*, a book by Al Jandl and Van Crouch. It was so obvious—just like faith for any area of life, it must have an expectation with it or it's dead. Planning for the increase and taking action is part of real faith. We immediately set up a church savings account. And before the end of the week, we opened an envelope from a non-church member that contained a $5,000 check in it with a note that read, "For your church building fund". Praise the Lord! We didn't yet have such a fund, but we had finally made a place for it. Now *that's* how a Kingdom principle works.

We can also apply the *Giving* principle to our *Savings* principle. First, we give to God. Second, we give to ourselves. *Ourselves* is our savings. It is our future. It is our investment plan. Third, we give to our bills. And lastly, we spend or give the rest. Many people have it totally backwards, so they start paying bills first. Many others have left out paying themselves altogether. But if we order our payouts by principle instead of by circumstance or emotion, we will soon find ourselves flowing in God's prosperity plan. Pay God first. Pay yourself second. Pay your bills third. And use the rest as you see fit. "Make all you can, save all you can, give all you can" (John Wesley). How much should we "pay" ourselves? How about 10 percent? How about a good healthy bit? How about at least *something* now and increase it later?

This is where many people have fallen victim to the reasoning of *I don't have any to save; I'm barely getting by as it is*. But that's what they said ten years ago as well, and for many, twenty and thirty years. There is never the perfect time to start saving. "He who observes the wind will not sow, and he who regards the clouds will not reap...In the morning sow your seed, and in the evening do not withhold your hand; for you do not know which will prosper..." (Ecclesiastes 11:4-6). If we try and wait for a future date, it seems to delay itself for so many reasons, *When I finally get a better job. After I pay off the car. Once I get married. When the kids are gone from the house. After we get the flat screen T.V. and surround sound. Once we accumulate some extra we'll invest it.* Or worst of all, *I just can't think about that right now.* And the reasoning just goes on and on. It's time that we acknowledge 'saving' as the will of God and start doing it by faith, securing this overlooked prosperity link.

What we need is the discipline of *deferred gratification*. Rather than obeying our lustful appetite for pleasure *now*, we should delay that gratification for later. Rather than gobble up our seed now, realize that seed invested right will grow exponentially for a much larger feast later. We'll need to overcome the fast food, fast pleasure, fast gratification lifestyle and realize that it sometimes contradicts Bible principle. Everyone could save something if they just gave some attention to it. Eliminate one Starbucks coffee or three small snacks from your weekly cycle. Funnel that $20 monthly savings into a time-proven investment strategy that follows God's "little by little" principle. And watch your holdings grow.

For example, if on the day of your child's birth, you took $20 and put it into a good "no-load" mutual fund, earning 8% to 10% average annual return, and if you continued that monthly for 65 years, your child could retire with about $1.2 million. The power of this is seen when you realize that over that 65 years, the total investment from your $20 per month was only $15,600. That's right. $15,600 turned into $1.2 million. (If the fund only earned the 8% annual average, the final amount would be $535,000...still pretty good!  Or smarter yet, increase the monthly amount to $50 at some point for a total around $2.5 million at 10%.)

Where does this power come from?  It comes from one of God's business system strategies called MATH. That's right, math *is* important after all. It's called *the time value of money*, or *compounded interest*. Too bad every brand new parent didn't know this, and too bad no one taught me this when I got my first job at age 16. If at age 16, a teenager gets a summer job and invests $2,100 into a no-load mutual fund that averages about 10% long term, and does this for five summers and then stops, his $10,500 investment will turn into over $1 million by age 65. Think of how his entire life would be different with a life-long consciousness that his retirement was secure. Think of what financial strength a person has when he's done right things early—how bold he can be in business decisions and how stable he can be all his life. There's power in saving and investing.

It is said that Albert Einstein was asked what he thought the greatest invention was. His answer was not the wheel or lever or some contraption. It was *compound interest.* Someone else said, "Compound interest is the eighth wonder of the world. He who understands it, earns it. He who doesn't understand it, pays it."

There is a scripture in the Bible that I've never liked at all, but I've taken it as a challenge. Jesus said that "the children of this world are in their generation wiser than the children of light. And I say unto you, make to yourselves friends of the mammon of unrighteousness" (Luke 16:9). I've never liked that first part. There's no reason why the world should be any wiser in this world's business system and investing system than those who know God. But every unsaved person who is faithfully funding their 401(k), 403(b), or IRA is exactly that—wiser than everyone who isn't. Making "mammon" your friend is not hard. It just takes a bit of attention, a bit of learning, and bit of discipline. We can't be lazy about putting our money to work for us.

This concept of saving and investing *little by little* (Proverbs 13:11) is completely separate and distinct from taking big risks and getting into complex investment deals. This Biblical model for increasing slowly but surely is all about passive investing a small portion each month, rather than large lump sum investing that carries more risk. And almost all wealthy people are using this model in some way, whether they realize it's Biblical or not.

When is the best time to plant a tree? Twenty years ago. When is the next best time to plant a tree? Right now. Do it now. Stop being shortsighted, and start your investing, little by little, *now*. Invest into yourself. Remember that we are willing to pay for whatever we value. Why not value *ourselves*? God values us. If we value ourselves, we will have no problem investing in ourselves—into our financial future.

Of course, there are many successful ways to invest money besides mutual funds, including rental properties, commodities, real estate, business start-ups and ownership, side sales, life insurance, and more. It's just that most of those either require much larger initial amounts to get started, or require much more time to manage, or include higher expenses, or carry more initial risk than passive, low-effort, mutual fund investing. And even if you are involved in several investment arenas, I would suggest also adding a mutual fund since it adheres to the Biblical, little-by-little, approach to saving money. And also because an IRA or Roth IRA mutual fund reduces your tax payments to the federal government and saves you money.

Whatever we do, we can't fall into the trap of "Well, I don't need to worry about it. I'll just trust God later in life." That's not very logical or Scriptural. If we can't even trust God for a little bit extra to save each month now, what makes us think we'll have strong enough faith later for some big provision in our later years? Why not start trusting God now rather than procrastinating the inevitable? If we don't ever save, how are we going to fulfill Proverbs 13:22, "A good man leaves an inheritance to his children's children"?

And be sure to catch this one tip:  set up automatic drafts from your bank account to fund your mutual funds.

Rather than make a new decision each month as to what to do with extra money, set up your investment funding on an automatic system, just like an employer transacted 401(k) would function. This is imperative for consistent investing. This prosperity link basically requires only a one time decision and then an annual review. And then you're in the will of God. If you disagree with the strategy of mutual funds and IRAs, fine, but don't throw out the principle. Find another successful way to save and invest little by little so that you're prosperity chain is connected.

# PROSPERITY LINK #6
# HARVEST

Alright, just a couple more links in the chain and we're ready to tighten it up and "pull 'er out". Next up is a law that will never cease—seedtime and harvest. It is a physical law and a spiritual law. Whatever we plant in the ground will come up, and whatever we plant in the Kingdom will come up. The seedtime part was covered in the *Giving* chapter, as all giving is counted for seed. However, many Christians would probably admit that though they've planted much seed in the past, it doesn't seem like the harvest they expected has come from it. And I believe this might be the reason. It's not that the seed has not grown. And it's not that the fruit has not sprouted and ripened. It's not that the harvest isn't sitting in the field. It's that people didn't know *how to reap it*, or that they didn't know they *had* to reap it.

Jesus said that in order to get harvest, we must *put in the sickle*.

> "The Kingdom of God is as if a man should scatter seed on the ground, and should sleep by night and rise by day, and the seed should sprout and grow, he himself does not know how. For the earth yields crops by itself: first the blade, then the head, after that the full grain in the head. But when the grain ripens, immediately *he puts in the sickle*, because the harvest has come" (Mark 4:26-29).

81

Reaping requires action.   In finances, it takes faith action.   To begin, let's get a mental image of the harvest fields.   Every time we honor God with our substance by giving to a church, a ministry, or to a person, it's like planting a seed in a field.   If we are consistent for a while in our giving, that seed turns into a row.   If we keep it up, those rows turn into a field, and fields turn into more fields. Picture it—for all believers who follow the seedtime principle, they have thousands of acres of crops that are maturing at all different phases of growth at any one time. Some are just seedlings.   Some are adolescent plants.   And some have mature fruit and are ready for harvest.   As long as we haven't skipped any of our seedtime seasons, we'll *always* have harvest seasons.   But for anyone who has let excuses stop them from sowing seed into the Kingdom for any period of time, they can fully expect some empty periods in the future.   Any time someone decides not to plant for whatever reason, good or bad, they are scheduling a season of lack for themselves sometime in the future.

On the other hand, if we are consistent in our giving, then we certainly have a field ready for the picking.   It just takes faith effort to get the fruit from the "field to the basket".   So we must grab the sickle and go.

Here is how to harvest.

First, I would say that there are two types of harvest. There is *daily* harvest.   And there is *exceptional* harvest.   We need faith for both.   Faith for daily harvest means that we lean on foundation scriptures for God being our Heavenly Father and providing our basic necessities every day.   We establish a relationship with God around the fact that every day, we get to "eat" without concern or worry.   Period.   We can use Matthew 6 for faith in that truth, or we can use Philippians 4:19 for it, or we can choose many other scriptures to build our faith in that Bible truth. But an active belief and thanksgiving toward God as our Source must be kept in our heart and mouth so that *normal* harvest from a *normal* work week will never cease. What we are looking for is a constant consciousness that all of our needs are met and that we have no doubt that God's "got it".

And next, we need faith for exceptional, uncommon and special surprise needs, desires, or raises that we want. We need access to daily money, but we also need faith for occasional *miracle* money. And faith for miracle money requires subsequent action. Sometimes it means asking, receiving, and thanking God. Sometimes it means declaring God's Word. Sometimes it means speaking directly to the thing of need and calling it in, using our God-given authority. And sometimes it means making a plan and moving forward by faith before anything is ever seen. And finally, once we are really in faith toward God for our exceptional harvest need, we'll act like it's so before it comes. Real faith moves forward like it's so.

When Israel and Judah teamed up against the Moabites, they found themselves in the battlefield with no water for themselves or their animals. They called for the prophet, who gave the word from God,

> "Thus says the LORD: Make this valley full of ditches. For thus says the LORD: You shall not see wind, nor shall you see rain; yet that valley shall be filled with water, so that you, your cattle, and your animals may drink...Now it happened in the morning, when the grain offering was offered,

that suddenly water came by way of Edom, and
the land was filled with water" (2 Kings 3:16-20).

Notice that before God could give the provision, His
people had to *dig the ditches*.   They had to devise the
opportunity and make a place for it.  If their faith in God's
word was real, they had to put action to it.  They had to
create the vision and prepare for the miracle.  So must we.
That's one reason why so few miracles happen for people.
They're praying hard about something.  But they're not really
expecting anything to happen or they would start moving
ahead with the plans.  If they really heard from God, and if
they really believed God, they would start "digging ditches"
for Him to fill instead of waiting to see the money first.

When the widow woman needed money to pay her
debts (2 Kings 4:2-7), Elisha was willing to work a miracle
on God's behalf.  He was about to create a huge batch of oil
so she could sell it and pay her debts, but he needed
something from the woman.  Before the supply can come,
there's got to be a receiver for it—something for it to fill.
The woman had to work first.  She had to collect the vessels.
And when the oil was poured into the vessels, it miraculously
continued until they ran out of vessels.  And then it stopped.
No more pots—no more miracle.  It's the same with us.
When we run out of opportunity, and when we run out of
expectancy, the supply ends.

God needs us to have a *vision* for the *provision*.  The
*pro*vision only comes to the vision.  *Pro* means 'in favor of'.
Without vision, there is nothing for God to be in favor of.
Without a design, or a business plan, or a final decision, or a
prayer of faith, or a firm direction, and movement toward it,
God has no interest in giving provision.

Putting in the sickle means that we put action toward a thing as if the money was already there. At Houston Faith Church, we've proved this out, time and time again. It began when we opened the church. We were seeking God on where to begin—in a school, in our home, or in a day-care? None of those seemed right. So, we began looking for our own retail or warehouse space to build out and have a complete set up. We found a perfect empty warehouse location that would seat about 100 people. It just seemed right. Our faith came from the inward witness I had when I had walked in the empty warehouse to check it out. And our faith was substantiated by a vision Joni had had previously of an empty warehouse. We knew God wanted us to have our own place, day one. So, without knowing who, if anyone, would join us in pioneering a church, we signed a five year lease for a total build-out of a brand new church interior before any church offerings ever came in. But then they did. After we made our decision, someone who wasn't even part of it gave us $5,000 to start. Then our church began, and the offerings came in. Since that initial faith decision over twelve years ago, Houston Faith Church has never missed rent, never missed one bill, and never missed payroll. We dug the ditch.

Each step requires a similar pattern. After a few years at church, Joni and I were the only ones doing all the office work, in addition to all the pastoral work. She handled the office administration, accounting and the operations. I handled all the audio, media, graphics, advertising, and products. And we needed help. But it didn't seem like we had enough income to hire someone. Then we remembered—there is never any provision until the vision comes. So we made the decision based on what was right and on what seemed right with the Lord, and we hired an assistant. And *bam*. Month one—offerings increased to the level we needed to pay someone. And it never ceased. Then employee number two—same scenario—not enough money beforehand, but we had to have another employee. Once again, immediate surprise increase in monthly offerings. And it wasn't just employees. When we contemplated an evangelism project or equipment purchase or media blast or whatever, there was no extra money until we put in the sickle, dug the ditch, or "stepped into the sea" like the Israelites who were sandwiched by army and water. Finally, on our third employee hire, we were keenly aware of how this worked, and I couldn't wait to hire the person and see how much the finances increased the next month. And God did it again— we had our largest offering month ever. And it never stopped. That's how to reap harvest using faith.

Don't ever let your financial situation dictate the plan of God for your life. It is the opposite. The plan of God should dictate the money. The decision we make and the ditch we dig will determine when God can give the supply. Remember, the *supply* is always for the *work*, "And God *is* able to make all grace abound toward you, that you, always having all sufficiency in all things, may have an abundance for every good work" (2 Corinthians 9:8). So plan the work and believe the supply in.

My first time to really petition God for some financial help was just after I had left my career as a consultant and began volunteering at my home church. My best friend from college was getting married and asked me to be in the wedding. So, I needed to rent a tuxedo. I needed money for a gift. And I needed money to play in the bachelor's golf outing (he knew I wouldn't be joining them for the night party, but he invited me to the day of sports). And the total amount I needed was $134. It sure doesn't seem like a lot now, but back then I didn't have it. When I left for full time ministry, part of my faith toward God included giving away all my available cash so that I wouldn't have a "plan B" to fall back on. So, I asked God for the $134 and thanked Him for it. That was the first week I ever received money in the mail. I opened an envelope that had $50 cash in it. *Glory to God.* I don't remember how the rest of the money came to me, but I sure remember the first $50 in my faith walk.

My second time to petition God for extra was one summer early in my preaching ministry, I had been given the opportunity to travel to New Jersey and New York for two ten-day R.W. Schambach tent crusades working with my friend and mentor, Angelo Mitropoulos. After praying it through, I knew it was the will of God for me to go, so I began making the travel arrangements and calculating the money I would need.

The total cost was $508, which I didn't really have. But since I knew what God wanted of me, standing in my kitchen, I simply asked Him for it. I believed it. I received it in prayer and thanked God for it. About fifteen minutes later, I walked to the mailbox out of my morning routine and discovered God's faithfulness once again. I had received a letter from my mom's friend which read, "Use this money for some place you'd like to travel this summer. Thanks for all your help." (I had been witnessing to one of her family members.) Enclosed was a check for $500 made out to my ministry. Wow. Glory to God. God had planned it all out.

He knew the end from the beginning. He knew I would obey His will. He knew I would ask Him. He knew I would believe the end He had declared. So He already had the check written for me. He met my need (of course, I had the last eight dollars). Did my faith matter? Yes, it did. Did making the reservations resemble "making this valley full of ditches"? Absolutely. I had to step out before the provision arrived. God knows ahead of time if we will seek Him, hear Him, believe Him, and step out. So, don't look at the natural circumstance to determine if and how God might fill the ditch with water. Notice that in that valley, the water came to Israel and Judah without a storm and without rain.

Another time God answered an exceptional harvest need for me was when I was asked by a pastor in Kenya to go preach his annual conference. One night after he asked a third time, I went outside to pray. I began my usual routine of praying in tongues and walking the neighborhood. I walked and meandered about thirty minutes from home, praying in tongues the whole time. After about an hour, it dawned on me that I had been praying about Kenya. It seemed as if I had prayed myself there and back, with all the details filled in. And I realized that was the plan of God. I chuckled a bit and thought, *Well, it looks like I'm going to Kenya*. For the next thirty minutes on my walk back to the house, I just thanked God and praised Him for His will. And then it hit me, *I'm going to need some money for this trip*. So, I quickly calculated in my mind how much I would need...and it totaled $1,800. I said, "Lord, I need $1,800." But God corrected me saying, "No, you need $2,500." I actually heard God say that down in my spirit. I replied, "Okay, Lord, I need $2,500. So I ask You for that now in

Jesus' Name." And that was the end of it. I had simply made the faith decision in my heart, and would soon be buying my ticket and packing. I walked in the house and went to bed.

The next morning was Sunday, and I went to my home church, not even thinking about the night before. After the church service, a brother in the church walked up to me and asked me, "Chas, are you believing God for some money?" I said, "I sure am." "How much?", he asked. "$2,500". He said, "I'll be back." He went to his wife and came back with a check for $2,500.

All I can say is that God is faithful to trigger the harvest once we provide the faith. And also, thank God for the brother who had his spiritual ear open. God is faithful to give the provision once we've decided on the vision and moved toward it. In this case, my determined decision was enough movement. *The miracle was in the movement.*

Clearly, there is something to this "ditch digging" and "putting in the sickle" that should curb our tendency to *only* *pray* about needs. Real faith acts. Real faith moves.

## Don't Trample or Pluck Up, But Protect Your Seed

Sometimes it feels like we don't have any harvest. Because the things of faith are invisible to the natural eye, we may feel like the seed we planted didn't come up. Maybe sometimes it didn't. Maybe some weird things were happening to our seed that we didn't realize were happening?

Maybe we've planted good seed, but we've not been careful with growing it. We give to God out of a cheerful heart, but we get home from work the next day and complain about our job. We worry about bills. And we walk around the house gloomy and murmuring *how we can't afford this and that*. We're trampling our seed! Or, we gave once, but we never watered our seed with further giving and by speaking quality words of life about our finances. It could happen. Until our mouth changes and stops speaking "doubt and death" over our situation, there is no harvest.

On the other hand, sometimes the harvest is there but we don't perceive it. In Mark 11, Jesus cursed the fig tree that wasn't bearing fruit as it should. But even so, it didn't appear that anything had happened. Not until the next day. The next day, the tree had clearly dried up from the roots. But at first, what was happening to the roots underground could not be seen, so it looked like Jesus' words carried no weight. But they did. Something was happening underneath.

Then Jesus taught His disciples, explaining that "…whoever says to this mountain, be removed and be cast into the sea, and does not doubt in his heart, but believes that those things he says will be done, he will have whatever he says" (Mark 11:23). Notice that whoever says it can *have what they say*. And notice what that person must believe. He must believe "those things he says will be done". It's not that we must get our heads around an entire mountain moving, but rather just believe that what we *say* matters. We must believe our words carry the authority. Whatever *I say* goes. Do we believe that for ourselves? When we do, we can make miracles happen. If words can begin the *death* of something at the root level, they can also begin a *miracle blessing* at the root level. So, ignore what you see at first, knowing that something's happening underneath.

People get stuck in their faith trying to move the mountain when really all they need to do is move their *mouth*. God's power is there, but it's not activated until we talk right. Miracles happen when our heart and mouth (our belief and our words) line up with God's Word. And until then, no need is going to move God. No begging, pleading, crying, balling or squalling about our finances is ever going to move God. God is always and only looking for faith—someone to believe and act like it.

So if we really believe it, we'll be happy. As a matter of *faith*, we're not even really *in* faith until we get happy. Faith is not about worrying until the answer comes and then getting happy. Faith gets happy and rejoices ahead of time, "...now you do not see Him, yet believing, you rejoice with joy inexpressible and full of glory" (1 Peter 1:8). Notice that even though the scripture is talking about Jesus, it's also giving us a principle of faith. By believing, we rejoice with *joy*. Believing God causes joy. Did you know that joy is the atmosphere for faith and miracles? Sometimes, when our money gets stuck and miracles seem far, and prayers have long flown away, it's simply time to rejoice. Harvest is out there in your field, and "putting in the sickle" can be as simple as getting a good celebration going on in your soul. Just force yourself to start praising God and thanking God and dancing around the house like the big ship already came in, and watch how fast the money pipe unclogs.

Our words create life or death, blessing or cursing (Proverbs 18:21). It is a known fact, even reported by local news authorities, that in the 1980s, Rev. Norvel Hayes saved his entire orange orchard with his words of faith.

> "God moved on me one morning and told me to buy a place on the side of a highway and make a mission out of it. It cost $90,000. Close to our mission, there is one subdivision called Beverly Hills, where about 7,000 retired people live. One time I was at the mission, and God showed me an orange grove with orange trees, laid out in rows on about 25 acres. God wanted me to buy it. A couple of years ago, a big freeze came to Florida. My orange grove was covered with snow, icicles hanging from the trees, limbs hanging all the way to the ground, loaded with ripe oranges in January. My neighbor had a grove right across the street from me that was in the same condition. If you know anything about citrus at all, you know that when this happens, you not only don't have any oranges, you don't have any trees. You might as well start knocking them down and planting a new grove. In the natural my orange grove was dead, all the trees. But...I believe God's power will do anything for you if you can believe it. So I just pulled my car up to my orange grove and sat there in the car by myself. I was afraid to take anybody with me because I was afraid they wouldn't believe it. When you want a miracle, you've got to get all unbelief away from you. So I went out by myself. I sat there and looked at that orange grove, icicles hanging off the branches, knowing in the natural that every tree was dead, never to bear another orange. I said, 'Lord Jesus, I obeyed You early one morning when Your Spirit came upon me and told me to buy this property,

start a mission, and work from door to door with these elderly people. I spent $90,000 buying this property, and I started a mission for You. And I thank You for every soul that's been saved. Now I believe You are a miracle worker and that Your power is available for me. I come to You, Heavenly Father, in Jesus' Name, and I bring this orange grove before You. I ask You to release Your miracle-working power from heaven and let it come and hover over every tree and protect it. And I say with my mouth that my trees will live and not die because Jesus said I can have whatever I say. I believe that Your power will protect my trees. Thank You, Lord.'

When I got through, I watched over the next three or four days as the sun popped out. The ice began to melt, and every orange on my trees fell off. Every leaf on my trees fell off. The same thing happened to my neighbor's trees. I kept saying, 'Thank You, Lord, for protecting my trees by Your mighty power.' About three or four weeks later it was time for the trees to start budding. Buds began to come out on all of my trees. Not on one of them. Not on 95 percent of them. I said on *all* of them! I sold 2,500 bushels of oranges! My neighbor's trees had died, and every other tree around there had died—except mine! I know God loves my neighbor, but my trees lived and his died. Why? Because I believed God for a miracle. I was in my neighbor's office one day, and he said to me, 'Mr. Hayes, you know it's amazing what happened. Your trees lived and mine died. Somebody told me you went up there in the snow and prayed. Is that true?' I said, 'Oh yeah. I went up there and prayed and asked God's power to come down over my trees and perform a miracle. God's got more power than a snowstorm and the Devil.' He said, 'I want to know how to do that. Do you mind if I borrow your tapes?' 'No, go ahead. I don't mind. You just read the Bible, that's all. You believe God is a miracle worker. It's that simple.' You see, even the orange experts can't understand what happened. But that's where God's power comes in. God releases an explosion of His power to give you a miracle if you need one, if you believe He's a miracle worker" (http://www.slideshare.net/FreeLeaks/endued-with-power-by-norvel-hayes-28686425).

Now that's how faith in God requires the power of our words in order to keep our harvest secure!

Angelo Mitropoulos told me a story of a time when his ministry finances seemed to dry up—doors were closing and nothing was in the mail. After things got quite uncomfortable, he and his wife, Christy, decided to pray. After a few moments, Angelo realized that Christy was falling asleep on the couch and he was barely even able to hear himself pray—just lethargic praying. But all of a sudden, he had an urge from the Spirit and he became flaming angry toward the devil. God revealed to him that the devil had set an operation against his finances. So, he stood up, and with bold authority, commanded Satan to loose his finances, and commanded the river to start flowing again. It took him about thirty seconds, and he knew they had the victory. And sure enough, the next day, the phone started ringing, doors started opening, and money showed up.

If the devil is messing with our money, we've got to catch him and deal with it. Just like when I once planted my tomato garden every year, the mockingbirds and blue jays would sneak in and peck my fruit to get the juice out. I had to take action and set up reflectors and "scare crows" or something to stop them. Likewise, if the devil is after our harvest, we stop him with our God-given authority. Catching and resisting the enemy is part of this link in God's supernatural prosperity chain.

For us to capitalize on our harvest, we're going to have to take action. We need to prepare for the increase. We need to dig the ditch. We need to be alert and protect our seed from danger. We need to call our harvest in. The fig tree apparently heard Jesus' words. So things that come out of the ground apparently have "ears". And since money is made up of something that comes out of the ground, money has "ears". So it can hear us when we call it in. (U.S. Money is actually made of 75 percent cotton and 25 percent linen, rather than from trees and paper, which some countries use.) If we start a business, we call in our clients and call in the cash. If we need some extra money here and there, we tell it to come in. And once we do it, know that "it will obey us" if we don't doubt. So, move on with the right plan and with full expectancy, and expect it to be so. Even though spiritual things like this may sound odd to the natural mind, that's what real faith does.

And finally, we need to stay determined and persistent. Good seed doesn't die. So, don't faint. No farmer in his right mind would ever plant a seed, get frustrated after a few days because nothing came up, and go pluck it up to see what happened. Why? Because he understands the principle of *seed* and *time*. Don't let the time between seed and harvest influence you to start saying dumb things. Don't start pressuring God with the date. Don't pressure people and start manipulating. Don't overwork this in your mind. Don't pressure yourself. Just let your faith grow the seed with steady expectancy.

No farmer would let his harvest rot in the field. He would put in the sickle and go for it. Realize that if you've been a giver in the past, you have a field that is ready for harvest when you need it. Hook up with God, get happy, and go for it. This dynamic link of putting in the sickle for harvest keeps the prosperity chain strong.

# PROSPERITY LINK #7
# WISDOM

Rarely do we find a wealthy person who isn't wise. Wisdom is essential for true Bible prosperity. It's essential in *obtaining* riches, and it's essential in *keeping* riches. Even if riches are a result of talent or fame, wisdom is still necessary to handle it. (Just think of how many multi-millionaires lose it as fast as they made it—lack of wisdom.) Wisdom is the principle thing (Proverbs 4:7), and if any man lacks this final link in the chain, he's commanded by God to get it.

What is wisdom? It is having good judgment, and it is being able to solve problems cognitively and rationally. Complete wisdom can handle both natural and spiritual matters. Wisdom can solve a daily problem at work, and wisdom can also assimilate a spiritual truth into a person's lifestyle. Wisdom knows how to use natural logic to make natural things happen, and wisdom knows how to use faith logic to cause supernatural things to happen. Wisdom is able to rightly prioritize life matters and accomplish them. And wisdom is able to not only see the value in spiritual principles, but also do them. (The wise man Jesus referred to, who built his house on a rock, was the one who heard the words of God *and did them* - Matthew 7:24.)

Knowledge, wisdom, and understanding are all important attributes of a successful life. *Knowledge* is the accumulation of facts and information (the *what*). *Wisdom* is the ability to use that knowledge effectively (the *how*).  And *understanding* is knowing how or why that solution actually worked (the *why*).  Knowledge, on its own, is somewhat dormant.  This is evidenced by some who have obtained several college degrees but can't keep a stable job.  I'm all for higher education—absolutely—but wisdom is the ingredient needed to assimilate that knowledge into real work situations.  Think of it this way:  knowledge is having a car key in your pocket.  Wisdom is putting the key into the ignition switch and turning it rather than just admiring it all day.  And understanding is the deeper knowledge of knowing what is happening under the hood to fire up the engine.

Wisdom is the ability to anticipate and solve problems.  It is the risk-assessor and opportunity-chooser for our financial options.  And it is the protection mechanism for our business decisions.  Wisdom extends even to our social skill set, being able to effectively communicate and relate to our fellow man in both business and personal situations.  Wisdom is more of a determining factor for wealth than is race, gender, or even education.  That's why many people without a college degree do better in business than people with one—it would most likely be because of wisdom.

But also, a wise person wouldn't neglect education carelessly.  Rather, wisdom allows a person to properly evaluate the need for education and not postpone it to enjoy the moment.  Wisdom allows a person to see beyond the barriers of family history, social stigmas, and personal intimidations about attaining higher education, and then do something.  And wisdom will enable a person to apply all the previous prosperity links into his or her life.

Notice in these seven links that there is none devoted to "spend less than you make". The reason is because operating under a balanced budget falls under the *wisdom* category. Wisdom will keep us out of trouble. Wisdom recognizes the burden that debt places on a family and takes unwavering steps to end "underwater" living. Certainly, borrowing money is necessary occasionally and is not a sin, but only if it's done with faith and with a legitimate plan of repayment. Carrying a reasonable house mortgage or a temporary and reasonable auto loan is fine. But carrying credit card debt is unwise. And "buy now pay later" is unwise. Basically, a wise person will recognize that all debt is a weight that burdens not only a family's cash flow but also their heart, and will therefore take precaution if acquiring it. Student loans are fine and necessary, but again, a logical plan is needed, and limits should be set. God's wisdom is available for every challenge. But if you're noticing a struggle in managing your money, it may be wise to seek out a good basic strategy such as Dave Ramsey's *Financial Peace University*.

How do we get wisdom? Either live a long time and go through the ups and downs of life, learning by experience. Basically, *get some grey hair*. Or ask God to give wisdom as from the Spirit of God.

> "If any of you lacks wisdom, let him ask of God, who gives to all liberally and without reproach, and it will be given to him. But let him ask in faith, with no doubting, for he who doubts is like a wave of the sea driven and tossed by the wind. For let not that man suppose that he will receive anything from the Lord; he is a double-minded man, unstable in all his ways" (James 1:5-8).

Notice that if we're going to ask God for wisdom, we must be confident that He will give it. And let's not reserve wisdom requests for emergency decisions only, where prayer turns into nervous desperation.   But, rather, let's make a determined and decisive pursuit of God for this intangible spiritual substance called *wisdom* until we are confident that it resides with us every day at all times in all things ("...and the [spirit of wisdom] shall rest upon Him" (Isaiah 11:2).

The challenge to us recognizing the need to pursue wisdom is that it's invisible to the naked eye and the undiscerning heart.   So, it takes humility and faith to acknowledge our lack of it and then actively pursue God to get it. But our happiness depends on it.

> "Happy is the man who finds wisdom, and the man who gains understanding; for her proceeds are better than the profits of silver, and her gain than fine gold.  She is more precious than rubies, and all the things you may desire cannot compare with her" (Proverbs 3:13-15).

> "I, wisdom, dwell with prudence... riches and honor are with me, enduring riches and righteousness.  My fruit is better than gold, yes, than fine gold, and my revenue than choice silver" (Proverbs 8:12-18).

Here's a good question for us all:  if given the choice, would we prefer a bucket of gold, silver, and rubies, or some wisdom?   Of course, we Bible-believers would make ourselves say, "wisdom".  But if it was a real option in front of us...well, let's just say we all need to ponder the real value we place on wisdom.  King Solomon did.  When Solomon took over the Kingdom of Israel from his father, King David, God wanted to show him favor and blessing, so he offered him anything he wanted.  Solomon didn't seem to hesitate as he looked at his life responsibilities, and rather than ask for riches or success or for God to solve some immediate problem he was facing, he asked for a wise and understanding heart to lead the nation well.  And God was pleased.  God told him that because he didn't ask selfishly, God would give him the wisdom, *plus* the riches and honor, "And I have also given you what you have not asked: both riches and honor, so that there shall not be anyone like you among the kings all your days" (1 Kings 3:13).  God was delighted to give prosperity.

But wisdom came first.

Some might read that story and think, *Yeah, but I'm not a king, and I'm not special like that.*  And that's part of the problem.  You *are* a king.  Jesus has *made* you a king and a priest unto Him (Revelation 1:6), giving you authority and position on this earth as an ambassador of Heaven.  And you are certainly special to God.  And more than that, God has commanded us to ask for wisdom.  We need it if we're going to fulfill God's plan for our lives.  So, do it.  Get wisdom, and give God a more qualified saint to work with.

Read the Bible.  It is full of wisdom tips.  Tips like: associate with right people (Psalm 1:1, 1 Corinthians 15:33), don't co-sign for family and friends (Proverbs 6:2, 17:18), save money for future opportunity (Proverbs 21:20), pay your debts and your taxes (Romans 13:8-10, Mark 12:17), and many more.

Wisdom will recognize and apply Bible virtues like endurance, persistence, and determination.  Even unsaved successful people have certain wise traits of diligence and never giving up.  Albert Einstein said that "Genius is 1 percent inspiration and 99 percent perspiration." Success always takes hard work. Einstein also said, "We often miss opportunity because it comes dressed in overalls and looks like work." Think about it. Thomas Edison failed in his first one thousand attempts at the light bulb invention. When a reporter asked him how it felt to fail one thousand times, he replied, "I have not failed. I have just found one thousand ways that don't work." Failure is not a problem. Failing to get back up and endure again is the problem. Wisdom knows the difference.

Henry Ford failed in his first five business attempts. But finally nailed it and gave us Model T's and Mustangs. "For a righteous man may fall seven times, and rise again" (Proverbs 24:16). Taking the promised land wasn't quick and easy for the Israelites, but they did it. One step at a time, one city at a time, one war at a time, they obtained their inheritance from God. I think part of today's problem is that people are too interested in only the "quicky" and go limp if there's any snag or hardship, so they miss God's covenant of prosperity.

A person with wisdom will recognize the value of being led by the Spirit of God and will develop his or her spirit man to do that. "For as many as are led by the Spirit of God, these are sons of God" (Romans 8:14). Wisdom will always remember to look for God's leading in all of our life activities and decisions. And that includes our financial decisions. What does it mean to be led by the Spirit? It means our mind, emotions, and body should not get the final say in our decision-making. It means we must get sensitive to the voice of God on the inside of us, which speaks to our spirit man. It means we must learn the value of the inward witness, which reveals God's will to us by way of unction and illumination and not usually by verbal sentences. "The spirit of a man is the lamp of the Lord" (Proverbs 20:27). When God wants to light our path, He lights our spirit rather than our mind. The trouble is that our minds are sometimes so strong and our spirits are so weak that we can't hear God. So it takes practice, and it takes developing our spirit man to a place that it can discern the leading of the Holy Spirit.

Taking the right job, moving to the right city, and knowing where to invest your time and money shouldn't be decided by a flip of a coin. And they shouldn't be decided by the carrot that someone has dangled, nor the advice from all your family experts, nor your theoretical statistical analysis. God knows the right step, and it's wise to wait until you hear Him.

There are many other applications for wisdom, for which the only way to be prepared is to have the wisdom ahead of time. So ask God for it. Get deeper in the things of God. It starts with a desire. And it starts with faith. Believe that you should get more wisdom, and then ask God for it. Money matters are never-ending, and your financial prosperity depends on you shoring this up in your life.

# PRAY FOR THE SPIRIT OF WISDOM UNTIL IT COMES

Here's a life-changing prayer you can pray for yourself. Paul prayed this prayer for the church at Ephesus to have the spirit of wisdom, but since it is in the Bible, it is a prayer approved by the Holy Spirit.  And it is extremely effective if you are diligent in your desire and pursuit.  When you pray it for yourself, make it personal and insert "I" and "my" for "you" and "your".  I pray,

> "...the Father of glory, may give to you the spirit of wisdom and revelation in the knowledge of Him, the eyes of your understanding being enlightened; that you may know what is the hope of His calling, what are the riches of the glory of His inheritance in the saints, and what is the exceeding greatness of His power toward us who believe, according to the working of His mighty power..." (Ephesians 1:17-19).

Notice the terms *'spirit of wisdom'* and *'revelation in the knowledge'* and *'eyes of your understanding being enlightened'*. Those spiritual things are the secret to your development in the Lord.  Pray it fervently until you see a change.  You can find similar prayers in Philippians 1 and Colossians 1.  And if you have been filled with the Spirit, pray in tongues a lot. Praying in tongues will enlarge your heart's capacity and help you tap into the spirit of wisdom.

Will you go after wisdom?  God is waiting.

# CONCLUSION
# WINDOWS OPEN, CHAIN CONNECTED, READY FOR BLESSING

Prosperity is based on principles. And for us believers, its source is God Almighty. He said He will "open for you the windows of heaven and pour out for you such blessing that there will not be room enough to receive it" (Malachi 3:10). It's clear, however, that He will not be pouring much if there are holes in the container. God doesn't mind spilling blessing off the top, but He does mind if it's squandered out of the bottom. To stay linked to God's prosperity covenant, it requires: 1) Getting rid of the poverty mentality, 2) Work, 3) Giving, 4) Not Worrying, 5) Saving and Investing, 6) Harvesting, and 7) Wisdom. All seven, all the time—there is no way around it.

God is certainly more concerned with our spiritual life, which is why we must focus on the internal, spiritual realities within us rather than the outward blessing. If not, then we're not prepared for prosperity anyway and there is no eternal blessing in it. Remember, we're laying up treasure in Heaven—not trying to achieve some earthly goal. So, if we do money right, in the will of God, by faith, and by principle, then we can have both.

If our soul does not fully comprehend that God is our source for all provision, then riches will sneak in as a counterfeit for God. Money solves a lot of problems, so if we haven't yet learned to trust God as our problem-solver, money begins to rise as our all-powerful one. And there is no blessing in that. Money has caused many people many sorrows. But if done God's way, "The blessing of the Lord makes one rich, and He adds no sorrow with it" (Proverbs 10:22).

There is a myth that spiritual people are not wealthy and should not be. And that wealthy people are not spiritual and also need not be. Both are wrong. Rather, we should all be spiritual, walk with God, and then operate in whatever financial grace we have and develop that grace with whatever faith we have. It would be feeble to go through this earth life as a believer and not partake of every last drop of the covenant inheritance we have in Christ, as it's already been purchased and fully provided—financial prosperity included.

But the paradox concerning financial abundance is to build our faith in it, fully expect it, rejoice in God about it, but *not* pursue it. Do things necessary to ensure it, stay faithful in all our dealings with it, but don't covet it, don't over-emphasize it, and don't love it. Let's seek only the Kingdom of God, seek only God's way of doing things, seek only the Lord, and keep our eyes solely on Him, the author and finisher of our faith. And it won't be long before out of the corner of our eye, surprisingly (but actually expected), supernaturally (but also somewhat naturally), excitingly (yet really more thankfully), we see our supply of wealth beginning to increase. And the fullness of prosperity will be ours as God provides an abundant supply for every good work He has called us to accomplish. So stay linked up to God, and He'll keep your "financial truck unstuck".

# ABOUT THE AUTHOR

**Rev. Chas Stevenson** is a Bible teacher and author of the life-changing book, *God, Why?*, the powerful inspirational book, *The Call of the Christian*, and the precise clarification book, *The Real Grace*. He and his wife, Joni are founders of *Stevenson Ministries* and are also founders and pastors of *Houston Faith Church*, an exciting and growing church in Houston, Texas. Chas' ministry to the Church at large is marked with a refreshing demonstration of God's Word and power that quiets the emotions, stirs the spirit, and brings people back to their high calling of God in Christ. With New Testament devotion to precise, scriptural logic, Chas is a foundation builder of God's Word in people, holding nothing back in igniting people's faith toward God while keeping them committed to the integrity of God's Word.

**Other Great Books** *from* Stevenson ministries

# God, Why? *book*

Why do bad things happen to good people?

Isn't it time to get the right answers about God's will and eliminate those big, nagging question marks around the subject of suffering, evil, and why bad things happen? Yes, it is time.

In God, Why? Chas Stevenson presents powerful, precise, scriptural logic that eradicates popular spiritual myths and flawed teaching about God's sovereignty that has misled and confused people about God's character and God's good will.

# The Call of the Christian *book*

Called...with a holy, significant supernatural assignment

Jump into this inspiring expedition of knowing God and doing exploits, where Chas shares the heart of the Father regarding your assignment - so that you can answer heaven's great trumpet call, *The Call of the Christian.*

Once you accept this call, your part in turning the world upside down with the gospel will be clear. And when you appear before the Lord Jesus at the last day, *"Well done, good and faithful servant..."* will be the words you hear.

# The Real Grace *book*

Solving the Grace Controversy

Either righteousness comes by obedience, or it comes by faith alone, but it cannot be both. Join Pastor Chas in this bridging of the gap where he explains how it is possible to "frustrate the grace of God" by pointing people back to law-keeping for righteousness and blessing, but also where it is possible to "fall short of the grace of God" by wrong doctrine and lifestyle.

For more products or information, visit us on the web.
www.StevensonMinistries.org
www.HoustonFaithChurch.org

Made in the USA
Columbia, SC
28 September 2024